Richard Parkinson

The experienced farmer

An entire new work. Vol. 1

Richard Parkinson

The experienced farmer
An entire new work. Vol. 1

ISBN/EAN: 9783337143268

Printed in Europe, USA, Canada, Australia, Japan

Cover: Foto ©Andreas Hilbeck / pixelio.de

More available books at **www.hansebooks.com**

THE
EXPERIENCED FARMER,

AN ENTIRE NEW WORK,

IN WHICH THE WHOLE SYSTEM OF

AGRICULTURE, HUSBANDRY,

AND

BREEDING OF CATTLE,

IS EXPLAINED AND COPIOUSLY ENLARGED UPON;

AND

THE BEST METHODS, WITH THE MOST RECENT
IMPROVEMENTS, POINTED OUT.

BY RICHARD PARKINSON,
OF DONCASTER IN THE COUNTY OF YORK.

IN TWO VOLUMES.
VOL. I.

PHILADELPHIA:
PRINTED BY CHARLES CIST,
NORTH SECOND-STREET.

1799.

TO

GENERAL WASHINGTON,

late PRESIDENT *of the*

UNITED STATES.

S I R,

To Dedicate, with propriety, a Work which treats of one of the moſt uſeful Branches of Human Induſtry and Speculation, ſomething more is required to exiſt in the object of the Addreſs than mere Wealth and nominal Superiority.

Liberality of Sentiment, extenſive Knowledge, and marked Philanthropy are the beſt claims to that deference and reſpect which

the

the Good afford with pleafure, and the Bad cannot withhold in juftice.

Known as you are, throughout the United States, for your enviable poffeffion of every one of thefe qualities, and equally diftinguifhed by your generous diffufion of an improved inheritance, I have in-fcribed to you the following Effay upon Agriculture, which you will receive with pleafure, becaufe it may be ufeful to the Community.

I have the honour to be,

SIR,

With the greateft refpect and deference,

Your moft devoted,

And obedient, humble fervant,

RD. PARKINSON.

SUBSCRIBERS' NAMES.

HIS Royal Highneſs the Prince of Wales
His Royal Highneſs the Duke of York
His Royal Highneſs the Duke of Clarence

A

Aſkam, R D. Mr. Knottingley, near Ferrybridge,
    Yorkſhire
Allot, J Eſq. Haigh Hall, near Pontefract, Do.
Alderſon, J. Mr. Dalton Brook, near Rotherham,
    Do.
Allenby, Charles, Eſq. Horncaſtle, Lincolnſhire
Armitage, Sir George Bart. L. L. D. Kirklees,
    Yorkſhire
Alderſon, Mr. Tickhill, Do.
Arlington, Rev. Swinhop, Lincolnſhire
Allenby, Samuel, Eſq. Maidenwell, Do.
Allenby, George, Eſq. Holbeach, Do.
Ailiſon, Mr. John
Akinſon, Mr. Joſeph, Levels, near Thorne,
    Yorkſhire
Addiſon, John, Eſq. Sudbury
Anſon, Thomas, Eſq. M. P. St. James's Street,
    London

B

His Grace the Duke of Bedford, three copies
Rt. Hon. Earl of Beſborough
Rt. Hon. Sir Joſeph Banks, Bart. K. B. LL. D.
    F.R.S.
Rt. Hon. Lord Bayning

Browne, Mr. Robert, Markle, near Haddington, Scotland

Burns, Mr. Robert, Markle, Do. Do.

Bell, J. T. Efq. Lincoln

Banks, Mr. Do.

Butt, W. Efq. New Bond Street, London

Beaumont, T. R. Efq. M. P. Bretton Hall, Yorkſhire

Boynton, Henry, Efq. Trin. Coll. Cambridge

Boomer, Jac. Efq. Rotherham, Yorkſhire

Beatſon, W. Efq. Do. Do.

Benſon, Mr. J. Thorne, Do.

Butler, Joſeph, Efq. Cheſterfield, Derbyſhire

Broadbelt, Mr. Robert, Thetford, Norfolk

Boyce, Mr. Charles, Rondham, Do.

Blyth, Mr. J. Louth, Lincolnſhire

Bateman, N. Mr. Killington, Yorkſhire

Bowns, Charles, Efq. Bank Top, Barnſley, Do.

Brackenbury, W. Efq. Clayton, Do.

Beale, Mr. Samuel, Miſſon, Do.

Barraclough, Mr. W. Shaftholm, near Doncaſter, Do.

Brackenbury, Rev. Edward, Skendleby, Lincolnſhire

Brackenbury, Richard, Efq. Aſwardby, Do.

Bourne, J. Efq. Dalby, Do.

Bourne, Mr. George, Haugh, Do.

Barber, R. N. Efq. near Lynn

Barker, Mr. Joſeph, Holbeach, Do.

Bell, Henry, Efq. Wallington, Lynn, Norfolk

Beymond, J. Efq. Trewer, Carmarthen

Blomefield, Mr. F. Swaffham

Biſh, Mr. John, Holbeach, Lincolnſhire

Browne, H. Efq. Lincoln

Barincher, R. N. Efq.
Booth, G. Efq. Wainfleet, Lincolnfhire
Bowles, W. Lifle, Efq. Donhead, St. Mary, Wilts
Brownell, Mr. J. Rotherham, Yorkfhire
Blyth, Mr. R. Doncafter, Do. two copies
Buckley, Mr. J. Normanton, Nottinghamfhire
Babb, Mr. Peter, Dalton Brook, Yorkfhire
Brookes, Mr. Ifaac, Herringheath, Bury, Suffolk
Bennett, J. Efq. Pitt Houfe, Wilts
Brandford, Mr. J. Godwick, Heakingham
Bagge, Thomas, Efq. Shadfet, Lynn, Norfolk
Bower, H. Efq. Emanuel College, Cambridge
Bradford, T. Efq. Woodlands, near Doncafter

C

The Rt. Hon. Earl of Chefterfield
The Rt. Hon. Earl of Carlifle, two Copies
The Rt. Hon. Earl Cholmondeley
Clarke, Mr. John, Barnby Moor, Nottinghamfhire
Clarke, John, Efq. Sheffield, Yorkfhire
Conyers, John, Efq. Mount Street, London
Chafe, Rev. W. Staverton, Northampton
Colbeck, Mr. John, Balby, Doncafter, Yorkfhire
Coltman, Thomas, Efq. Hornby, near Horncaftle
Cartwright, Charles, Efq. Marnham, Notts
Chriftian, Mr. Benjamin, Burleigh, near Stamford
Caffon, Mr. W. Stubbs Hall, Yorkfhire
Cooke, Bryan, Efq. M. P. Ouftone, Do.
Cowlam, Mr. Samuel, Crowle, Lincoln
Childers, C. W. Efq. Cantley, Yorkfhire
Champion, Mr. W. Workfop, Nottinghamfhire
Chorley, Edmund, M. D. Doncafter, Yorkfhire

Cooke, John, Efq. Swinton, Yorkſhire
Cooke, Rev. George, Sprodbro', Do.
Cartwright, Mr. Thomas, Ulceby, Lincolnſhire
Cracroft, Thomas, Efq. Weſt Keal, Do.
Clough, Mr. R. M. Gayton, near Louth, **Do.**
Clarke, C. M. Efq. Louth Do.
Codd, Richard, Efq. Do. Do.
Connington, James, Efq. Horncaſtle, **Do.**
Clitherow, Mr. Richard, Do. Do.
Cartwright, Capt. Edmund, Brothertoft, **Do.**
Coke, T. W. Efq. M. P. Holkham, Norfolk, two
    copies
Colhoun, W. Efq. M. P. Wrotham, Do.
Clarke, Edward, Efq. M. P. Wimbledon, Surry
Crewe, J. Efq. M. P. Grofvenor Square, London
Clowes, John, Efq. near Lynn
Cooke, Mr. Henry, Lincoln
Cracroft, T. Efq. Weſt Keal, Lincolnſhire
Copley, Thomas, Efq. Doncaſter, Yorkſhire
Cheſter, Mr. W. Thorne, Do.
Cutfortha, ———, Efq. Rotherham, **Do.**
Colman, Mr. Thomas, Thorne, Do.
Cooke, John, Mr. Lincoln
Cooke, Sir George, Bart. Wheatley, Yorkſhire
Cooke, George, Efq. Streethorpe, Do.
Count La Tour du Pin, Greffin Hall, Norfolk
Crew, John, Efq. M. P. Crew Hall, Cheſbire
Cracroft, John, Efq. Hackthorne, near Lincoln

D

His Grace the Duke of Devonſhire
The Rt. Hon. Viſcount Admiral Duncan
Dodds, Mr. Thomas, Scotland

Davis, John, Efq. Loughbro', Leicefter
Deane, M. Efq. No. 1, Walton Place, Blackfriars Bridge, two Copies
Dudley, Rev. H. B. Bradwell Lodge, Suffex
Downs, J. Efq. Staverton, Northamptonfhire
Dickins, Rev. W. Do. Do.
Deakin, Mr. Jofeph, Tinfley, Yorkfhire
Dunhill, John, Efq. Mayor of Doncafter, Do.
Drummond, Rev. G. H. Rawmarfh, Do.
Denton, Mr. John, Ferrybridge, Do.
Dunhill, Mr. W. Grantham, Lincoinfhire
Deighton, Mr. John, Cambridge
Day, Mr. Robert, Doncafter, Yorkfhire
Dunhill, Mr. Rich. Newton near Doncafter, Do.
Danfer, Mr. H. Barnfley, Do.
Drake, Mr. T. Hobbis, Norfolk
Dalton, Henry, Efq. Gainfbro', Lincolnfhire
Dawfon, Mr. W. Tadcafter, Yorkfhire
Duncombe, T. Efq. Thurcroft, Do. two Copies
Duncombe, C. S. Efq. Duncombe Park, Do.
Deal J. J. Efq. Sharton, Dorfet
Davis, Mr. J. Pall Mall, London

E.

The Rt. Hon. Earl of Egremont
The Rt. Hon. Earl of Effingham
Earnfhaw, Mr. F. Roole
Elmhirft, W. Efq, Ouflethwaite, Yorkfhire
Elmhirft, W. Efq. Stainby, Lincolnfhire
Elliot, Mr. John, Uffelby, Do.
Everfon, John, Efq. Holbeach, Do.
Evans, Mr. W. Narbeth, Pembroke
Evelyn, Sir Frederick, Bart. Wooton, Surry
Earl, Mr. Thomas Ayre, St. Laurence

F

The Rt. Hon. Earl Fitzwilliam
The Rt. Hon. Earl Fortescue
Foster, Mr. Thomas, Scausby, Yorkshire
Fawkes, F. Esq. Barmbro' Grange, Do.
Firth, Mr. A. Rawmarsh, Do.
Foster, Mr. T. jun. Doncaster, Do.
Frost, Mr. John, Windsor, Berkshire
Foster, Mr. John, Brampton, Yorkshire
Faulder, Mr. John, Sebergham, Cumberland
Fisher, Thomas, Bawtry, Yorkshire
Frank, Bacon, Esq. Campsall, Yorkshire
Foljambe, F. F. Esq. Osberton, Do.
Foljambe, J. S. Esq. Aldwark, Do.
Fydell, Thomas, Esq. M. P. Botton
Folkes, Sir M. Bart. M. P. Hillington Hall, Norf.
Fiddy, Mr. J.
Fountain, Mr. ———, Norwich
Fair, Charles, Esq. Jedburgh, Scotland
Fen, Thomas, Esq. Sudbury.

G.

The Rt. Hon. Lord Gwydir
The Rt. Hon. Lord Grantley
The Hon. R. F. Greville, M. P.
Greville, H. F. Esq. Skelbroke Park, Yorkshire
Gray, Mr. Owen, March, Cambridgeshire
Grose, Daniel, Esq. F. A. S.
Green, J. Esq. Cridling Park, Yorkshire
Garlick, W. Esq. Dodsworth, Do.
Garland, W. Esq. Woodhall, Do.
Gibbeson, R. senior, Esq. Lincoln

Gili, Mr. J. Excife Officer, Doncafter
Gordon, ———, Efq. Kew Green
Green, Mr. Thomas, Bentley, near Doncafter
Graburn, Mr. W. Barton, Lincolnfhire
Gilby, Mr. John, Alford, Do.
Gaze, Mr. L. Saltfleetby, Do.
Gurney, Bartlet, Efq. Banker, Norwich
Gofling, Francis, Efq. Do. London.
George, G. B. Efq. near Lynn
Gotterfon, Mr. John, Houghton, Norfolk
Grefham, Mr. John, Barnaby, Do.
Grant, Mr. John, Wickham, Lincolnfhire
Grove, Thomas, Efq. Fen Houfe, Wilts
Goldem, Mr. M. Bury, Suffolk
Guife, Sir William, Bart. Higham, Gloucefter

H.

The Rt. Hon. Lord Hawke, L. L. D.
The Rt. Hon. Lord Harewood
Sir Car. Haggerftone, Bart.
Lady Haggerftone
Sir Gilbert Heathcote, Bart. M. P.
Hay, Robert, Efq. Scotland
Holt, Rt. Efq. Stongton, Leicefterfhire
Harris, John, Efq. Bruen, Oxon
Harris, Thomas, Efq. Belmont, Middlefex
Hall, Mr. John, jun. Iciles, Rotherham, Yorkfhire
Harrifon, H. B. Efq. Daventry, Northamptonfhire
Hides, Mr. Samuel, Tathwell, Lincolnfhire
Holland, S. Efq. Tenbury, Worcefter
Hall, Mr. J. Ferrybridge, Yorkfhire
Hopkinfon, F. Efq. Worcefter
Hewitt, N. W. N. Efq. Belham Houfe, York

Hardy, Mr. J. North Witham, Lincolnshire
Higgins, Godfrey, Esq. Skellow Grange, York
Hepworth, Mr. J. Bramwith, Do.
Hassell, J. Esq. Hull, Do.
Harneis Theo. Esq. Hawciby Lincolnshire
Halifax, Mr. W. Gayton, Do.
Hudson, Mr. John, Ashby Thorpe, Do.
Hodgson. Mr. John, Saltfleetby, Do.
Holbins, Mr. Henry, Nottingham
Holman, Edm. Esq. Downham, Norfolk
Hide, John, Esq. Lexham Hall, Norfolk
Hayward, Mr. W. Sudbury
Hammond, Anthony, Esq. Westacre, Do.
Hughes, J. W. Esq. Hegil, Carmarthen
Howel, John, Esq. Carmarthen
Hill, Mr. John, Lexham, Norfolk
Hobbes, T. D. Esq. Norwich
Handley, Benj. Esq. Sleaford, Lincolnshire
Heald, Rd. Esq. Horncastle
Hutton, W. Esq. near Gainsbro'
Hammond, Mr. Thomas, Whiston, Yorkshire
Hedges, Rev. Mr. Thryberg, Do.
Hawton, Mr. Andrew, Scotland
Harrison, John, Esq. Norton Place
Honywood, Sir John, Bart. Evington, Kent
Hartley, —— Esq. Christ Coll. Cambridge
Holt, Mr. R. Langton, Leicestershire

J

Jerningham, Sir Will. Bart. Gressin, Norf. 2 Cop.
Jenkinson, Mr. Thomas, Holbeach, Lincolnshire
Johnson, Mr. Thomas, Crowle, Do.
Johnson, John, Esq. Sandtoft Grove, Do.

Jones, W. Efq. Carmarthen
Johnfon, Mr. John, Kempton
Ingleby, Mr. W. Cheadly, Staffordfhire
Johnftone, Rev. Mr. Ely Place
Jackfon, Rev. Gilbert, D. D. Donhead, St. Mary's

K

The Rt. Hon. Earl of Kinnoul
Knightley, Sir J. Fawfley Hall, Northamptonfhire
Knightly, Rev. T. Charlton, Do.
Kent, Nathaniel, Efq. Craig's Court, London
Kelly, W. Efq. Charles Street, Weftminfter
Kirkham, Mr. John, Hagnaby, Lincolnfhire
King, Mr. John, Swaffham
Key, Mr. John, Holbeach
Kay, J. L. Efq. No. 10. Dover Street, Piccadilly

L

The Hon. Edw. Lafcelles, M. P. Harewood Houfe
The Hon. Hen. Lafcelles, Efq. M. P. Do.
Layton, Mr. William, Putney
Lewin, Mr. Robert, Long Acre, London
Leathes, S. Efq. Cornhill, Do.
Lee, James, Efq. Carlton, Yorkfhire
Lee, William, Efq. Grove, Do.
Loxley, Mr. W. Sprodbro', Do.
Lloyd, John, Mr. Bielfby, Lincolnfhire
Lee, Sir W. Bart. Hartwell, Buckinghamfhire
Linton, John, Efq. Freeftone
Letherland, Col. John Street, Adelphi, London
Lowe, Rt. Efq. Oxton
Lifle, Rev. W. B. D. St. Mary's, Wilts
Lawes, Mr. W. Sharton, Dorfet
Lay, Mr. James, Snettifhham
Legard, Digby, Efq.

M

The Rt. Hon. Earl of Mansfield
The Rt. Hon. Lord Melbourne
The Rt. Hon. Lord Mexborough
Malatrot, Mr. J. Doncaster, three Copies
Mackie, Mr. W. Scotland
Mott, Mr. John, America
Mellifh, Henry, Efq. Cullumpton, Devon
M'Dowell, Mr. Edm. New Bond Street, London
Molyneux, Sir F. Bart. LL. D. Wellow, Notts
Mackafon, Mr. Egham, Surry
Maffingberd, T. Efq. Candlefby, Lincolnfhire
Moody, Mr. Geo. Gringley, Nottinghamfhire
Mitten, Mr. W. Badfworth, Do.
Martin, J. Efq. Sandall, Yorkfhire
Marfhall, W. Efq. Theddlethorp, Lincolnfhire
Meeds, Mr. Edward, Mavis Enderby, Do.
Maffingberd, C. B. Efq. Ormefby, Do.
Milnes, R. S. Efq. M. P. Fryftone, Yorkfhire
Maclean, L. M. D. Sudbury, Suffolk
Macauley, F. Efq. Clough Houfe, Huddersfield
Micklethwaite, John, Efq. Hilboro', near Lynn
Mawkinfon, Mr. W. Holbeach, Lincolnfhire
Mingay, Mr. Thomas, No. 8, Smithfield, London
Money, Capt. Walthamftow
Mills, John, Efq. Great Queen Street, Weftminfter

N

Newton, Charles, Efq. Rotherham, Yorkfhire
Northey, W. Efq. Queen Street, May Fair, London
Northey, W. Efq. Mortimer Street, London
Nelthorpe, J. Efq. Grimfby Hall, Lincolnfhire
Newbold, S. Efq. Sheffield, Yorkfhire
Nevile, Syer, Rev. Great Walding, Suffolk

O

Orton, T. Efq. March, Cambridgefhire
Oxley, Mr. John, Rotherham, Yorkfhire
Oftliffe, Mr. Scarthing Moor, Nottinghamfhire
Overton, Henry, Efq. Loverfall, Yorkfhire
Oftler, Mr. R. Aylefby Caiftor, Lincolnfhire
Oakes, Orbell Ray, Efq. Bury, Suffolk
Ogden, Edm. Efq. Caftle Hill, Dorfetfhire
O'Kelly, J. Efq. Cannons

P

The Rt. Hon. Earl Poulett
Parkin, Mr. Rotherham, Yorkfhire
Parkhurft, J. G. Efq. Hutton Lodge, Do.
Parkhurft, C. Efq. Henrietta St. CavendifhSquare
Prince, Mr. George, Salford, Worcefterfhire
Pollen, G. A. Efq. M. P. LittleBookham, Surry
Parker, J. Efq. Sheffield, Yorkfhire
Paffmore, Mr. Thomas, Sheffield, Yorkfhire
Philips, Mr. Edward, Towcefter
Parker, Hugh, Efq. near Sheffield
Peech, Mr. Samuel, Sheffield, Yorkfhire
Parkin, Mr. Sheffield, Do.
Parkinfon, Mr. J. jun. Afgafby, Lincolnfhire
Payne, W. Efq. Frickley, Yorkfhire
Pilkington, Sir Thomas, Bart. Chevir, Do.
Parifh, Mr. J. Harrington, Lincolnfhire
Pegge, Mr. Andrew, Scotland
Pennel, Skelly, Efq. two Copies
Paddy, Rev. Mr. Kelling
Palmer, Mr. Samuel, Holbeach
Powell, J. W. Efq. Lynn, Norfolk

Price, Barrington, Esq. Beckets, near Farrington

R.

His Grace the Duke of Rutland
Rennie, Mr. Geo. Fantasie, Scotland
Royles, Mr. Mansfield, Nottinghamshire
Robinson, Robert, Esq. Kensington
Roberts, Mr. J. Fetter Lane, London
Ross, Maj. Gen.
Raynes, F Esq. Stonehill, Nottinghamshire
Randall, James, Esq. Basten, Kent
Robinson, John, Esq. Windsor
Ramsden, T. Esq. Hampole
Ramsden, Sir John, Byram, Yorkshire
Richardson, W. Esq. Limber, Lincoln
Rinder, Mr. J. Towes, near Louth, Do.
Rockliffe, Rev. Francis, West Ashby, Do.
Rockliffe, Mr. Samuel, Do. Do.
Rinder, Mr. Robert, Skendleby, Do.
Royce, Mr. John, Woodhamwalter, Essex
Rowbotham, Mr. W. Holbeach, Lincolnshire
Roe, Mr. John, Worksop, Nottinghamshire
Ramsden, Rd. Esq. Blamley, Leeds
Robinson, Mr. John, Doncaster
Ramsden, Rt. Esq. Carlton, Nottinghamshire
Rutter, Mr. Epsom, Surry

S.

The Rt Hon. Earl of Scarborough
Sir John Sinclair, Bart. LL.D. two Copies
Seaton, Mr. Ger. Reedness, Yorkshire
Sotheron, Col. Pontefract, ditto
Stanhope, W. S. Esq. Cannon Hall, York

Sayle, Mr. B. Wentbridge, ditto
Smith, Mr.
Shirreff, Mr. J. Scotland
Savers, Mr. Alex. ditto
Somerſville, Mr. A. ditto
Stone, Mr. I. P. Loughborough
Swincy, Mr. F. Stafford
Smith, Mr. J. Margaret-Street, London
Seaton, W. Eſq. Cuckfield
Spooner, W. Eſq. Rotherham, Yorkſhire
Smith, J. Eſq. Holbeck, Leeds
Squire, Thomrs, Eſq. Peterborough
Sturtle, Mr. J. Witham-Common
Sebright, Sir J. Bart. Beachwood, Herts
Stanley, Mr. Rd. Rotherham, Yorkſhire
Staniforth, Mr. Sheffield, Ditto
Sayle, Mr. B. jun. Brightſide, Ditto
Skelton, Mr. Britwait, Ditto
Sitwell, Sitwell, Eſq. Reniſhaw, Derbyſhire
Spurr, Mr. J. Yews, near Doncaſter, York
Rt. Hon. Lord Sefton
Rt. Hon. Lord Somerville, P. B. A.
Sampſon, Mr. John, Langton, LincolnſhireWilts
Syer, Rev. Neville, Great Waldingfield, Suffolk
Scrope, J. Eſq. Long Sutton, Lincolnſhire
Styleman, H. Eſq. Snettiſham, Norfolk
Smith, Mr. J. J. Michael-Grove, Suſſex
Shelly, Sir John, Bart.
Stanton, Mr. W. Cuckfield, Ditto
Slator, Mr. William, Holbeach, Lincolnſhire
Spencer, Mr. Rt. Hodſick
Rt. Hon. Lord Stourton, Stourton-Houſe, York
Shillito, Mr. M. Beale, Ditto
Shillito, Mr. J. Urldale, Ditto

Shillito, Mr. John, Ickworth-Park, Suffolk
Simpson, Rev. J. Hemsworth, Yorkshire
Swallow, Mr. Rd. Selby, Yorkshire
Stone, Mr. Crook, Norfolk, near Lynn
Sawyer, Mr. J. Headlesey
Smith, Mr. R. Lound, Nottinghamshire
Steel, Mr. J. Wooton
Shaw, Jos. Esq. Epsom, Surry
Sanxter, Mr. W. Horseheath

T.

The Most Noble the Marquis of Townshend
The Rt. Hon. Lord Teynham
Taylor, Mr. J. Canklow, Yorkshire ; a Member of the Russia Agriculture Society, St. Petersburgh, two Copies
Taylor, Mr. James, Treaten, Yorkshire
Taylor, Mr. Richard, Letwell, Ditto
Tooker, Samuel, Esq. Rotherham, Ditto
Thorpe, William, Esq. Gauber-Hall, Ditto
Thelluson, P. J. Esq. M. P. Rendlesham, Suffolk
Taylor Mr. Jo. two Copies
Taylor, Mr. John, Letwell
Thew, Mr. Richard, jun. Wrangle
Tudor, Henry, Esq. Sheffield, Yorkshire
Tatham, E. Dr. Rector of Lincoln Coll. Oxford
Travelyars, W. B. Esq. St. John's Coll. Camb.

V

Vollands, Rev. William, Hemsworth, Yorkshire
Veary, Mr. Wickham
Vyner, Rt. Esq. M. P. Gautby, Lincolnshire
Vipan, Benj. Esq. Southeray, near Market Downham

U.

Underwood, Mr. W. Melton Mowbray

W.

Wafhington, General, Mount Vernon, America
The Rt. Hon. Earl of Winchelfea
Wright, John, Efq. Doncafter, Yorkfhire
Wilkie, James, Efq. Scotland
Walker, Mr. F. Ditto
Wikinfon, Mr. T. Ridge, near Skyms
White, George, Efq. Newington-Houfe
White, John, Efq. Soho-Square, London
Whitehead, Mr. John, Whifton, Yorkfhire
Willan, J. Efq. Hatton-Garden, London
Willock, J. Efq. Golden-Square, Ditto
Walker, Jof. Efq. Eaftwood, Yorkfhire
Walker, John, Efq. Rotherham, Ditto
Walker, Thomas, Efq. Wencobank, Ditto
Walker Samuel, Efq. Mafborough, Ditto
Walker, J. Efq. Clifton, Ditto
Whitelock, Mr. J. Brotherton, Yorkfhire, 2 Cop.
Ward, St. Andrew, Efq. Hutton Pagnel, Ditto.
Wood, Mr. George, Lincoln
Webfter, Mr. Jofeph, Levels, Yorkfhire
Winn, Sir Rowland, Bart. Noftell, Ditto
Wentworth, G. W. Efq. Wooley, Ditto
White, Mr. W. Norwich
Wrightfon, W. Efq. Cufworth, Ditto
Wroughton, Geo. Efq. Adwick, Ditto
Woodcock, T. Efq. Doncafter, Ditto
Wilkinfon, E. Efq. Potterton Lodge, Ditto
Wilfon, C. Efq. Elmfall Lodge, Ditto
Woodyeare, John, Efq. Crookhill, Ditto.
Walker, Mr. W. Doncafter, Ditto

Wilkinson, Rev. W. Grasby, Lincolnshire
Whitworth, Mr. G. Beelsby, Ditto
Walls, Rev. E. Boothby, Ditto
Wood, Mr. R. Tathwell, Ditto
Wood, W. Esq. Thoresby, Ditto
Wright, Mr. Philip, Spilsby, Ditto
Waldegrave, Rt. Esq. Bennington, Ditto
Watson, Edward, Esq. Kirton Fen, Ditto
Wainman, Oglethorpe, M. D. Wisbeach
Waller, T. M. Esq. Norwich
Waite, Mr. No. 2, Old Bond Street, London
Wiberforce, W. Esq. M. P. Hull
Walker, J. E. Esq. Lynn, Norfolk
Waterson, Rev. Edward, Sleaford, Lincolnshire
Wray, Sir Cecil, Bart. Sumner Castle, Ditto
Wrangham, Rev. Fran. Hunmanby, Yorkshire
Walsh, Mr. J.
Wright, W. Esq. Edinburgh
Weir, Mr. Peter, Ferrygate
White, Mr. Moorfields, London
Winship, Mr. J. Beelsby, Lincolnshire
Wardlow, Henry, Esq. Cromer, Norfolk
White, Mr. W. Norwich
The Rt. Hon. Henry Willoughby

Y

The Rt. Hon. Lord Yarborough, two Copies
Young, Arthur, Mr. S. B. A.
Youle, Rev. A. Retford, Nottinghashire
Yarborough, Mrs. Campsall, Yorkshire

INTRO-

INTRODUCTION.

THINKING it neceffary, for the fatisfaction of thofe who may perufe the following fheets, to fay fomething of myfelf, and of the means by which I acquired that knowledge of farming in general which is now fubmitted to a candid Public; I fit down to write this Introduction, which contains a concife account of my own life, fo far as refpects the different occupations of a farmer, and of a breeder of all forts of ftock.

My father rented a farm called *Aby-Grange*, fituate near Alford, in the county of Lincoln, which confifted of about 400 acres; a clay foil, much of it very poor land, chiefly ufed for the purpofe of breeding fheep, horfes, beafts, pigs, &c.

My father was famed for the beſt breed of black horſes—horſes of moſt action and greateſt power. The horned cattle were of a very good mixed breed, well inclined to feed. We uſed to draw eight pair of oxen to do the farming buſineſs, and kept what may be termed a large dairy. The ſheep, at one time, if not the beſt, were certainly not much inferior to the beſt in this iſland. I ſpeak of a period long before Mr. Bakewell's famous breed, which is ſuppoſed to have been produced from the ſtock of Mr. Stow, of Bilſby, about four miles from the place of my birth. My father hired rams of Mr. Stow. We had very good pigs. Of graſs-land my father was an excellent manager; by his great attention to ſurface-draining, he converted a farm remarkable for rotting ſheep into a perfectly ſound and thriving paſture. As a proof of this, he did not in the laſt thirty years loſe a ſcore of ſheep, although in one year there was a general rot all over the iſland; but in that year he did not loſe more than ſix, or *ſeven* at the moſt.

My father had a farm at Salfleetby, one at Truſthorpe, and another at Skegneſt: theſe three farms were all in what is termed the MARSHES, and conſiſted entirely of graſs-land.

It

It may, perhaps, convey some useful knowledge, to inform the reader of the purposes to which these farms were applied.

The *fresh*-water marshes were proper for feeding cattle and sheep, and were far from being bad for horses. The *salt* marshes were much better for horses, and excellent for old sheep. Upon horses they act as physic, and at the same time make them fat; but they are improper and unwholesome for steers, and for all *young* stock, except horses. Lambs feeding on them will purge to death, whilst a *young* horse will thrive in a most astonishing manner.

My father employed every means in his power to instruct me thoroughly in the business he practised with so much success, and neglected no opportunity of gratifying the ardent desire he had of making me a complete farmer; and the strong propensity he thought he discovered in me, at a very early age, for the profession, encouraged him to persevere in his endeavours.

He made me assist in performing every part of the farming-business from the time I was able until I quitted him; and the experience I gained thus early from my own observations, joined to the instructions of my father, enabled me when very young, to be a tolerably good

judge

judge of the different forts of foil our feveral farms were compofed of.

The *Marfhes* lay fome miles diftant from the home farm; and one part of my province being the driving ftock to and from them, it frequently fell in my way to hear from others opinions of the ftock I was attending, my father being noted for good ftock. Thofe opinions I carefully liftened to, and certainly profited by; as I had afterwards the opportunity of afcertaining the value of them, and whether they were given with judgment, by feeing how the ftock turned out, and how they fed.

I alfo examined, with a minute degree of attention, the management of the different farms I paffed; which from the flow pace the ftock travelled, I had ample opportunity of doing.

My father took me a farm (of Mr. Vyner of Gautby) at Claythorpe, diftant about a mile from our houfe. Mr. Vyner being very averfe to ploughing, it was with much difficulty he was prevailed upon to fuffer me to plough forty acres; but by this improvement I was enabled to keep nineteen fcore of fheep upon the farm, that never before had maintained a greater number than thirteen fcore—a very material difference. I likewife kept many more beafts

and

and horfes than the old farmer my predeceffor; befides raifing a quantity of corn.

Four years afterwards I went to Afgafby, near Horncaftle, in the county of Lincoln. This farm was unfavourable for ftock of any kind; what were kept there required confiderable affiftance from art; as nature would of herfelf, in that fituation, furnifh but a fcanty allowance. It confifted of four hundred acres of land, with right of common over the very extenfive and valuable commons of the eaft and weft fens. And here I acquired, though at a heavy expence, a thorough knowledge of the advantages and difadvantages of pafturing on commons. The plough-land of this farm confifted in general of clay, with flints on the furface, covering a ftratum of white clay, intermixed with a fmall quantity of fand and flint.

The methods purfued in agriculture, at that period of time, were turnips, barley, clover, and wheat; and that rotation of crops is in fome places yet, though injudicioufly, perfevered in.

I well knew the value of *manure*, and felt the want of it—confequently ufed every means within the compafs of my knowledge to procure it. I formed fuch a refervoir, or receptacle

tacle, for the moiſture of the fold-yard, as is deſcribed in the body of this work: but I totally neglected the advantage of the *green crop,* the fold, and ſtall-feeding in ſummer; which would have increaſed the quantity of manure full *one third*—an acquiſition of conſiderable conſequence, independent of the ſaving in the food of the animals ſo kept. By ſuch increaſe of manure, and the diſtribution of it as recommended in this work, my farm would have been much more profitable.

During eight years' reſidence on this laſt-mentioned farm, I became acquainted with the firſt and moſt reſpectable breeders of ſheep in the county: Mr. Chaplin, of Tathwell; Mr. Bourne, of Dalby; Mr. Codd, of Ranby; and ſeveral others.

With Mr. Chaplin I became particularly intimate; and he introduced me to Mr. Bakewell, by prevailing upon me to go to view the ſtock at Diſhley, and to hire a particular ram for him for the ſeaſon. Glad of the opportunity of converſing with a man of Mr. Bakewell's experience and acknowledged abilities, I with pleaſure accepted the commiſſion.

My ideas of ſtock at that time were, that none were valuable but what were large. I

had

had that feafon confiderably enhanced the value of my own ftock (though in the time of the
American war, when ftock of all forts fetched
a low price), as I proved by the fale of fome
drape-ewes. The average prices were from
fix to feven fhillings per head, even of thofe by
the moft famous breeders in the county. But
one hundred of mine were purchafed of me, by
Mr. Fydell of Bofton, at fifteen fhillings per head,
with forty culls at thirteen fhillings per head.

I had the vanity to confider myfelf the firft
in rank as a breeder of fheep. It was not therefore extraordinary for a man who entertained
fo extravagant an opinion of himfelf, to glance
fuperficially over the ftock of another; who,
from the envious difpofition too common in
mankind, had many detractors amongft male-
volent and interefted competitors. I am obliged
to own (what now feems almoft incredible to
myfelf) I looked upon Mr. Bakewell's fheep
with indifference, if not contempt. The firft
objects pointed out to me as worthy of notice,
were eight tups, three heifers and calves, on a
piece of land near the houfe; but they appeared to me fo fmall, that I beftowed no more
attention upon them than juft to perceive they
were

were beasts and sheep. I was shewn more rams, and behaved with the same cool indifference. I next got amongst the breeding ewes. With them were some extraordinarily large Flanders mares, of a beautiful jet black, with remarkably long manes and tails : these caught my eye—their appearance struck me forcibly ; but for the mares, I might have passed over the most valuable breed of sheep in this kingdom without noticing them ; so totally were my ideas taken up by the *large ram* I had come in quest of. Stopping to look at the mares, some ewes attracted my notice. I requested the liberty of touching them ; which was readily complied with. The ewes were immediately put in a fold, that I might examine them at leisure. According to my usual custom, I began with the best, and was much surprised at the perfection of the sheep ; but how shall I express my astonishment at not being able, after *touching* the greatest part, to find a *poor* one amongst them ! I awoke as from a sound sleep, and was ashamed of my stupidity. I discovered, in an instant, the sheep of Mr. Bakewell to be far superior to my own, which I had, until that moment, thought some of the best in the kingdom.

My

My curiofity was ftimulated. I requefted
to be fhewn the whole farm, having repeatedly
been told that Mr. Bakewell's fheep were put
into particular paftures for *fhew* only, but that
there were other paftures into which they were
turned at night to feed ; and being rather afhamed of my carelefsnefs at the outfet, I determined to beftow a minute examination upon
every part of Mr. Bakewell's management that
I fhould have the opportunity of infpecting
during my ftay.

The paftures in which the breeding ewes juft
mentioned were, being much beaten by the
Flanders mares and the young beafts, would
no doubt juftify the fufpicion that the ftock
were only put in them for the purpofe of fhew.
Before that time I had no idea of fuch thrift, or
fuch difparity in the animals feeding. The
largeft of my own ftock were the fatteft ; I
thought this to be the cafe every where.

In going over the farm, I faw other animals
valuable as the fheep in proportion : there
were fome yellow cows, by far furpaffing any I
had before feen, beautiful in the extreme, and
uncommonly fat. The cabbages were un-
touched,

touched, the carrots unpulled, turnips unftock-
ed, the eddifh uneaten ; a convincing circumftance that no deception was ufed in their
feeding.

Returning towards the houfe, I perceived
whence the idle and malicious tales refpecting
Mr. Bakewell originated ; and where lay the
miftake of thofe who, without malice, had
propagated the ftories. On a fmall piece of
land were ten fheep, fix beafts, and feveral
horfes, all feeding on green fodder ! This was
a novelty to me.

I had not yet feen the principal object of
my journey, the great ram : of courfe I was
obliged to enquire particularly concerning him.
Immediately my curiofity was gratified with a
fight of that extraordinary creature, who
appeared to me to be of the *Tees-Water*
kind, with but a fmall ftrain of the *Difhley*
in him.

In the fame pafture with the ram were feveral
of the largeft ewes I had ever feen, and fome
wethers, all of the *Tees-Water* kind.

In my return I faw fome fmall rams, which
I examined with care : one, a very fmall one,
I took a particular fancy to.

I dined

I dined with Mr. Bakewell, and during four hours converfation with him, obtained more ufeful knowledge with refpect to the breeding and management of ftock, than I had been able to acquire during all the time I had practifed the bufinefs of a farmer. It is with gratitude I acknowledge the obligations heaped upon me by that great, that intelligent, that ufeful man ; and I hope the precepts he afterwards took fo much pains to inftill into me, will prove beneficial to the public.

I hired the large ram, and likewife one of Mr. Bakewell's own breeding. They were much efteemed and admired by all good judges in our neighbourhood.

This journey totally removed many pernicious prejudices from my mind ; and from a conviction of my error, I acquired the habit of not trufting too implicitly to appearances and to my own preconceived opinion ; which was of great advantage to me in my refearches after ufeful knowledge.

I left Afgalby, and went to Doncafter ; where I foon after took a farm, which may truly be called an *experimental* one. A great many of the experiments there made are defcribed in
this

this work. I was greatly encouraged to perfevere in my improvements, by the attention shewn me by Sir John Sinclair, Bart. President of the Board of Agriculture. That very useful and intelligent man, Mr. Robert Brown of Murkle in Scotland, had come to take a view of the agriculture of the west riding of Yorkshire. To him I got introduced ; and he, conceiving a favourable opinion of my knowledge of rural economy, recommended me to Sir John, who soon after did me the honour of calling upon me. Sir John was so good as to send me some reports of the state of agriculture in the Lothians, &c. and some other instructive publications; the perusal of which raised my ideas, and excited my curiosity so much, that I was not satisfied until I examined the modes of farming practised there and in other parts of England and Scotland.—The result of my observations, and of my own experiments, I have detailed in the following Treatise.

I now must make an apology to the reader for having dwelt so long upon myself and my own concerns, which I trust his candour will not impute to egotism—I despise the character of an egotist : I only wished to point out the

sources

fources whence I derived my knowledge of the science I mean to treat of.—The height of my ambition is to be ufeful, and to convey my thoughts in fuch a plain, familiar ftyle, as fhall be perfectly intelligible to the practical farmer.

THE

EXPERIENCED FARMER.

SECTION I.

Method of making Fallows by having a Crop at the same time, and sometimes Two Crops, with a Crop of Wheat the succeeding year.

ON A CLAY SOIL.

First year. A pea fallow, drilled and manured.

Second year. Wheat.

Third year. Beans, drilled and manured.

Fourth year. Either wheat or barley.

Fifth year. Clover with a *top-dressing*.

Sixth year, Wheat.

This is what I term a rotation of crops; and by manuring once in two years, each crop may be expected to turn out a good one. To purchase manure (which in many situations cannot be obtained) will not be necessary; as, from

the

the fucceffion of crops laid down, the land's own produce will fupply a fufficiency. By mowing the ftubble, throwing the roots and weeds into the refervoir (as will be defcribed hereafter) you will procure *four loads* of good manure per acre each time for the two drill crops, and fix loads of *top-dreffing* for the clover; making together fourteen loads per acre for the fix years on an average. If there be a redundancy of manure, the overplus may be laid on the clover. The bean crop might perhaps take more manure than here allowed: but peafe will not bear a larger quantity, as they would be liable to run to ftraw and yield but little. Should beans rife too high, it will be neceffary to top them with a fcythe in a ftraight fhaft; which is done at a trifling expence. But if garden beans be fown, they will not be liable to fhoot too fpindling, as they require richer land.

When rape feed fells well, a crop might be thrown into this fort of land; but although rape be in general reckoned profitable, in this inftance it could not turn to much greater account, fuppofing a good return; for rape takes two years to produce a crop on fallow lands, in the old hufbandry. It muft be fown in the
month

month of Auguft, and will not be fit for reaping until the following July or Auguft twelve
months; confequently from the profit muft be
deducted two years rent, as the land lies idle fo
long to receive its crop and take its fallow.
On frefh or fward lands intended to be pared
and burned in the months of June and July, it
is certainly very proper and profitable to fow
rape.

SECTION II.

A regular Rotation of Crops on different Soils,
demonftrating what the different Soils are by
Nature intended for.

ON A DEEP LOAM OR WHARP.

FIRST year. The potatoe-fallow, manured,
will turn out the moft profitable.

Second year. Wheat.

Third year. Drill beans, manured; or peafe.

Fourth year. Barley.

Fifth year. Clover, manured.

Sixth year. Wheat.

Rape might be fown on this land to advantage after the crop of peafe, if podded; and
inftead of barley as before hinted. If rape be

sown and reaped for feed, the ftraw muft be carefully ftacked up, to be ufed in the ftall or fold as litter for cattle. The ftalks and roots muft be all removed carefully from the land, and carried into the fold-yard, that the cattle may tread upon them all winter. By thefe means a great deal of manure will be gained, as they will imbibe the urine of the cattle; and the wheat crop will be better for the refufe being taken away.

On a Sandy Soil.

Firft year. Turnip fallow, drilled and manured.

Second year. Barley; or wheat, if the turnips are early eaten off.

Third year. Peafe, drilled and manured. The fame year, Turnips in drills, if the peafe be podded.

Fourth year. Barley.

Fifth year. Clover, manured.

Sixth year. Wheat.

The drill crops fhould have four loads of manure each; and the clover, as foon as the barley is removed, fix loads of manure or compoft.

On

On a Lime-stone Soil.

First year. Turnip fallow, drilled and manured.

Second year. Barley.

Third year. Pease, drilled and manured.

Fourth year. Wheat.

Fifth year. Clover, manured.

Sixth year. Wheat.

By way of crofs-cropping, if the fourth crop were oats, it would be full as proper, and useful; fome oats being generally wanted on a farm.

On Moor Land, or Peat.

First and Second year. Rape for feed, with a dreffing of lime.

Third year. Wheat.

Fourth year. Drilled and manured pease or beans.

Fifth year. Wheat.

Sixth year. Oats.

On a Poor Sandy Soil.

First year. Fallow turnips, drilled and manured.

Second year, Barley.

Third year. Seeds, to be eaten by sheep for three succeffive years: but if once mown, to be eaten by sheep the other two years, and then sown with wheat or rye. This crop ought to be dibbled.

On a Poor Limeftone.

Firft year. Turnips drilled and manured.
Second year. Barley.

Third year. Seeds, mown, or eaten by sheep, the next two years—then sown with wheat or oats dibbled.

As the two laft fpecies of foil may be fuppofed not capable of bearing a conftant rotation or fucceffion of crops, they may be ufeful for breeding or feeding sheep: the foil will be enriched by keeping them upon it; and if, the laft year of the feeds, the farmer beftow a top-dreffing of manure, from his refervoir of compoft prepared for that ufe, of from four to fix loads per acre; the benefit of fuch dreffing will appear in the wheat crop, and repay him well.

N. B. The manure will proceed from the barley crop and firft year's feeds' mowing.

Loofe Gravelly Soil

muft be treated in the fame manner as poor fand. There are fome moor lands which are fandy, and confequently proper to be eaten by fheep, in the fame manner as the two former foils, if they do not rot them.

N. B. The mode and expence of preparing land for thefe crops will be explained in Section XLV.

SECTION III.

The proper method of making Manure, and bringing it with defpatch to the greateft degree of perfection; fo that the whole quantity may be put on the Land the fame Seafon, and Crops immediately grow thereon.

ALL fold-manure ought to be moved from the fold every *month* or *fix weeks*. By letting it lie longer, the cattle will tread it fo hard in fome places as to prevent the regular putrefaction; and if there come dry weather in the fpring months, it will rot only *partially*, and not *equally:* and it is a very defirable quality in manure to rot. It is therefore neceffary to carry the whole from the fold-yard, and to throw it up in hills, fo that the rain and fnow may penetrate freely; which will caufe the manure to ferment, and the fermentation produced by the heat of the dunghill will deftroy the

feeds

feeds of noxious weeds as effectually as if they were boiled in water, and will render them as incapable of vegetation as if they had lain twelve months in a hill.

It has been customary with some farmers, intelligent men in other respects, to turn their manure over in the fold, in the spring, in dry weather; and as it is dry and trodden down hard, they are obliged to cut it with a hay-knife, and throw it up in lumps: but, in heating, the dry part will injure the moist, and prevent putrefaction. That, therefore, is not so good a method; for the more it is shaken about, and the lighter the hill is made, the quicker it heats and rots: and no fold-manure can be in a proper state to be laid on land till it has undergone a degree of fermentation. The manure thrown out at stable-doors, if the cattle do not tread it down, may change into a proper state without being moved. The greater variety in the forts of manure, the better; such as the dung of pigs, horses, cows, &c.

By this method you may, in one or two months, make excellent manure, far exceeding that made by the common procefs, which requires so much time and labour to bring it to perfection. The *old* farmer prides himself on

having

having manure accumulated for a year at leaft preceding the ufe: but he is wrong to boaft of fuch management—it is falfe economy. The falts and oil, which conftitute the richeft part of the manure, evaporate; and the juices drain from it, if it lie long after being taken from the fold-yard or refervoir.

When roots of grafs, couch, ftubble-roots, rotten vegetables of moft forts, weeds from ftanding pools and ditches, and almoft all kinds of refufe ftuff, by being plunged in the refervoir, are made into manure, it will take much longer time to rot it down; as, from its being made chiefly of weeds, and roots of weeds, they will be liable to grow again, efpecially if there be any couch-roots among them.

Let the manure from the refervoir be worked down very fine, and, when compofed of roots of weeds, laid as a *top-dreffing* on clover or feeds two years eaten; for, were it put in drills, and covered with mould, there is danger of its again filling the land with weeds. It is well known the fmalleft piece of couch-grafs will, from its great fucculency, be liable to vegetate. I tried an experiment, by raking the couch clean from from the fallow in very hot dry weather, and had it carried into the fold-yard, where at the

time

time upwards of one hundred pigs were, and continued feeding during the whole of the summer, which was remarkably dry. The couch was of course much turned over by the rooting of the pigs. During the course of the winter it was covered with horse-dung, cow-dung, and a variety of matters by the different stock turned in, and by manure carried from the stables and cow-houses; and it remained in the fold-yard eleven months, and was afterwards used on the land set with potatoes. A small quantity of the couch, notwithstanding, sprouted amongst the potatoes.

Another very good mode of making manure (of which some experiments have been tried under my direction) is, by driving sheep out of the fold where they have been folded, to eat turnips in the day, and putting them at night into a straw-fold, made purposely for sheep. This not only answers the purpose of making manure, but also causes the sheep to feed quicker and confume less turnip; for when sheep leave turnips, they will eat *straw* by way of variety—as a well-fed citizen will devour a decent quantity of pudding after a few pounds of beef. Sheep lying in the fold littered with straw, find themselves much more comfortable

than

than on a cold dirty layer, where turnips have been eaten off by them; and were thefe fheep continued in the field, as many of them as could would creep into the hedge-bottoms for fhelter, and there drop much of their manure, which would be totally loft to the ufe of the land.

For greater conveniency, you may make a fold in fome place near the turnip-field; carry the ftraw into the fold, and put the fheep into it.

It is proper to roufe the fheep and ftir them about in the fold before they are driven abroad in the morning. By this means they empty themfelves; and thus diforders incident to fheep at turnip may be frequently prevented, and a quantity of dung is faved which otherwife would be loft on the road to the turnip-field. I know a farmer who, by following the above rules, has this feafon made a confiderable quantity of manure of an excellent quality.

By attending to the above directions, manure in high perfection may be made in fix weeks or two months; and, inftead of lying, according to the old cuftom, on the high roads, in hedge bottoms, fold-yards, &c. may, by drill-hufbandry, be depofited in the land, and good crops of peafe, potatoes, beans, cabbages, turnips, &c. be growing thereon.

SECTION IV.

By Drill-Hufbandry, four Loads of Manure, properly managed and applied, will anfwer the purpofe of fixteen Loads in the old Way of Hufbandry.

BY drills being made two feet afunder, and the drill fix inches wide at the bottom, there will be juft one fourth part of the ground covered with manure. Now, as fix inches multiplied by four gives two feet, which will be the diftance from drill to drill, and as four multiplied by four makes fixteen, it follows, that if the whole of the land had been covered with manure, fixteen loads would have been required for what is as fully and beneficially performed by four; that is, by one quarter of the quantity ufed by the old method of dreffing, fuppofing it of the fame thicknefs and quality: and, as in the drills it is fo clofely laid in the earth, and the feed fown upon it, the crop receives the whole of the benefit.

It

It will be generally agreed, that beans, peafe, cabbages, &c. are by this method allowed a proper fpace to bring them to the greateft perfection, and a fufficient quantity of manure to promote a ftrong vegetation : but by fpreading only four loads of manure in the old way, and fowing the feed broad-caft, the farmer will find himfelf greatly deficient in yield of CORN, weight of turnips, cabbages, &c. compared with the crop produced by the new fyftem.

Another great advantage attending my method is, that the crop will have double earth to grow in, and that the land may be cleaned at the fame time it is growing, and bear a much better crop of wheat afterwards. Many other benefits will arife from the ufe of this drill hufbandry. By putting the manure in as here directed, the fun is prevented from exhaling moft of its fine fubtile parts, fo conducive to the nourifhment of the plant : the earth, by covering the manure, receives all the juices the manure is capable of beftowing : whereas, by throwing or fpreading it about upon the land, perhaps the feed falls in one place, and in another the manure, which the fun and wind dries to fuch a degree that it becomes like ftraw again, as the fcantinefs of the crop too often makes evident.

SECTION

SECTION V.

Method of making Drills, and putting Manure in them.

THE beſt method of making the drill is with the Rotherham or ſwing-plough, by drawing a furrow down the land, then coming back without any furrow to the place you began at, and beginning there and drawing, by the ſide of the firſt furrow, another furrrow twenty-four inches diſtant, in the manner land is wreſt-baulked, and then coming up the firſt furrow again. The firſt drill is then finiſhed. By this method the plough makes an open ridge, ſo as properly to contain the manure. When this is done throughout the field, or as much of it as you chooſe; then, to put the manure in the drills, let the horſes go up one drill; and the cart-wheels up the two others. Going along the drills in this manner will injure them but little. The man in the cart may, if required, throw from the ſame ſtation manure into nine drills. The load of manure ſhould be ſuch as to go through the field in a ſtraight line; as turning round with the cart would ſpoil the drills: therefore no more drills muſt be manured than the load will go through with. My

cuſtom

cuſtom is to have one man on the cart, and a woman, or boys and girls, to ſpread the manure regularly along the drills. This is a good method of proceeding. It is very eaſy to count the number of drills contained in an acre of land; and thus, if your carts are regularly filled, every acre of ground will be manured in an equal manner, which is not eaſily done by the old method.

SECTION VI.

Beſt Method of treating each Crop; with the Seaſon for Sowing and Reaping.

THE wheat crop may be ſown from September to January with nearly equal ſucceſs. Late ſowing in ſome parts has anſwered ſo well, that many farmers have ſown ſo late as February; but, in general, November will be found to be the beſt month; except where lands are liable to be flooded in the winter. That ſort of land ſhould be ſown as early as poſſible; becauſe, if the plants get weaned from the kernel, and take hold of the earth for ſupport, water may continue upon them a long time, without much injuring them. But, if the land were flooded before the wheat comes up, it would be totally deſtroyed.

Land

Land liable to be flooded fhould be fown with a drill, for the following reafons: If a wet winter be fucceeded by a dry fpring, the foil will become fo hard as very much to impede the progrefs of the plant; and when rain falls, it penetrates the earth but partially. Were the fcarifier and horfe-hoe ufed, it would lighten the foil, and the rain would penetrate more generally.

The fort of land we are now fpeaking of is very apt to abound with what is called fpry-grafs—a fpecies of grafs which comes up fo thick as to make abfolute fwards of the fpots it grows in, which are generally the moifteft parts of the field. This kind of grafs robs the wheat-plants of their food or nutriment: and where it abounds, you muft expect but a fcanty crop of corn. As a remedy for this evil, fow the feed-wheat in drills. and in the interval betwixt drill and drill fcarify or horfe-hoe the land; which will deftroy the grafs and weeds growing in the intervals, and pulverife the foil fo as to receive freely and equally the rain and dews. The wheat may be moulded by the hoe; which will make the plants vigorous, enable them quickly to cover and protect the ground from the effects of drought, and enfure the fuccefs of the crop. It would likewife be a great faving

towards

towards cleaning the land for the next year in the bean-fallow ; for such land may be conftantly managed, as above directed, with beans, and wheat.

This kind of land is likewife liable to crack, and to gape fo wide as to receive, to a confiderable depth, the foot of a horfe, and confequently make it dangerous for man or beaft to walk over it. The pulverizing it in the manner before mentioned, would in a great meafure prevent the cracking.

Where the old fyftem is followed, beans very often fail of producing on this foil a good crop, owing to too much or too little moifture while growing. Oats profper on fome of this fort of land ; and a crop of oats may be taken after wheat, when the land is in good condition ; but I do not approve of fuch cropping. Before the bean-fallow, the beans muft be drilled and manured ; and if you beftow *fix loads* per acre in the drills, as before defcribed, the land will be far lefs liable to crack ; for, by moulding the beans, they will foon acquire ftrength and fize fufficient to fhelter the land, and by keeping it fhaded prevent its cracking. In my opinion, peas are more proper than beans for land fo circumftanced ; as, by lying

down

down, they cover the ground more clofely and
preferve a greater degree of moifture : but if
you have a bean crop, and the beans run up
too high, it will be advifable to top them with
a fcythe in a ftraight fhaft. A man would top
them for fix pence per acre; and the operation
would make them bear better.

I muft repeat my predilection for peas on
land liable to be flooded, as they are much
fooner ripe ; and the fhorter the time the crop
is on the land, the lefs the danger of lofs by
fuch floods : therefore the earlier the peas the
better. I fee no reafon againft fowing garden-
peas generally. I have always found them to
produce the greateft crop ; and if ufed, they
would be equally cheap to the grower for feed,
and furely more profitable, as they would boil,
grind, into flour, and turn to great advantage
by being gathered green at the beginning of
fummer. Befides, as they are early off the
land, it might be fcarified to make as perfect a
fallow as the farmer could defire. By fuch a
fucceffion of crops, the ftraw, ftubble, &c.
would produce fufficient manure to furnifh at
leaft fix loads per acre every two years.

I cannot advife the fowing of clover, or of
any of the grafs-feeds, on this land, except
wanted

wanted for pasture or meadow. If the soil here spoken of, viz. clay, have had a large quantity of lime on it, there is no doubt but the lime may have injured it, and you may expect the ground to crack much, as most sorts of lime impoverish land.

A *sandy* soil, or a *lime-stone*, is not difficult to till, being of a kinder nature than stiff clay. I found that the best time for sowing wheat on these soils was the month of November ; and the wetter the land, the more likely you are to succeed. But if the land be clean, I do not recommend scarifying the wheat in the spring ; but prefer treading with sheep early in that season. Bush harrowing and rolling answer well on these kinds of soil.

Peas may be sown, if the weather prove favourable, soon after Christmas. A month or six weeks difference in the time of sowing is not very material ; but if sown early, the crop will be sooner ripe, and equally productive. You may stir the mould about them till May : and by doing so you will keep the ground as clear of weeds as if the peas had been sown late. Even in the month of May they may be sown with advantage, if your land cannot be put in a proper condition before.

VOL. I.   E   Beans

Beans may be fown in February, and until April. Barley is beft fown in March : late fowing of barley makes the grain fmall and coarfe, and much inferior to that fown early : however, it may be fown from March to May. Oats may be fown from March to May. Clover-feed is beft fown with barley or oats, and harrowed in, as are all other feeds intended for fward, &c. Bufh-harrowing is a good way where feeds are fown.

Having fpoken particularly as to the times of fowing, it may be neceffary to fay fomething generally as to the times both of *fowing* and of *reaping* ; for, as fituations and feafons, which are the guides to both, vary fo much, no precife rules can be abfolutely laid down for either the one or the other. But one general obfervation may be made : Corn fown early is moft likely to fucceed, by having more time for tillering or branching, and from being fooner ready for reaping. Early fowing has fo many advantages over the late, that, in my own practice, I have experienced a difference of one third in the amount of the produce, by the difference of a few days in fowing, upon land fimilar in every refpect. Without doubt, it is beft to be as early as the feafon and the nature of the intended crop will admit of.

SECTION

SECTION VII.

The Method of scarifying and making Land fit for Wheat after the other Crops are off.

BY putting the manure, as before directed, into drills two feet asunder, it becomes necessary to cross the drills to mix the manure well in the soil, and to pulverise it. The readiest way to do this is, by Cook's scarifier : but those who are not in possession of that useful machine, may substitute one of a simple construction, which will be described hereafter. Ploughing in this case is very improper. For if there be a small quantity of couch-grass, or of any other weed, the plough turns it downwards, causes it to spread abundantly, and hides it ; so that, when you come to plough for sowing wheat, the weeds are set at liberty again to sprout out at a season when no weeds die. Cook's scarifier draws out the roots of the couch-grass at full length. The plough would cut them up, and turn them over, and consequently increase the number of roots ; the smallest bit of which will grow. By the scarifier all other weeds, such as thistles, &c. are cut up, and, when harrowed, are easily collected together and carried off.

Strong

Strong clay-land, when in drills, may be scarified, when a plough in a dry season would have no good effect, not even touch it in the old way of cultivating land. Cross-ploughing of fallows, though so frequently practised, is a most pernicious custom; for, if it were possible to desire a crop of couch-grass, ploughing in that manner, and harrowing after without raking up the refuse, would most effectually answer the purpose.

SECTION VIII.

A Calculation of Six Years Expences of the Drill-Husbandry, according to the New System, and of the Old, shewing the Disbursements for each.

OLD SYSTEM.	NEW SYSTEM.
First year, Fallow.	*First year, Turnips.*

	£.	s.	d.		£.	s.	d.
Four ploughings and harrowings at 6s. each,	1	4	0	Ploughing an inch and half deep, - 0		4	0
Twelve loads of manure at 8. per load,	4	16	0	Harrowing and raking, rolling, &c. 0		3	6
				Ploughing twice, harrowing, raking, &c. 0		13	0
				Leading off refuse, 0		1	0
				Seed and sowing, - 0		1	6
				Making of drills, - 0		2	6
				Three times ploughing the turnips, and hoeing, - - - - 0		8	6
				Six loads of manure, at 8s. per load, - 2		8	0

£6	0	0	£4	2	0

OLD SYSTEM.	£. s. d.	NEW SYSTEM.	£. s. d.
Brought over - - -	6 0 0	Brought over - - -	4 2 0

OLD SYSTEM.

£. s. d.

Brought over - - - 6 0 0

Second year, Barley.

Ploughing, harrowing, and sowing, 0 6 6
Weeding the crop, 0 0 6

Third year, Beans.

Ploughing, harrowing, and sowing 0 6 6
Weeding, - - - - - 0 0 6

Fourth year, Fallow.

Ploughing three times
and harrowing, 6s.
each time, - - - 0 18 0

Fifth year, Wheat.

Ploughing and sowing, - - - - - - 0 6 0
Weeding, - - - - 0 0 6

Sixth year, Oats.

Ploughing and sowing, - - - - - - 0 6 6
Weeding, - - - - 0 0 6

£.8 5 6

NEW SYSTEM.

£. s. d.

Brought over - - - 4 2 0

Second year, Barley.

Ploughing and sowing, harrowing, &c. 0 6 6
Weeding, - - - - - 0 0 3

Third year, Beans or Peas.

Two ploughings harrowing, raking, &c. 0 13 0
Drill making, - - - 0 2 6
Four loads manure,
at 8s per load, - 1 12 0
Three times ploughing, to mould the
peas and destroy the
weeds, - - - - - 0 4 9
Leading off refuse, 0 1 0

Fourth year, Wheat.

Scarifying, - - - - 0 2 6
Ploughing, sowing &c. 0 6 0
Weeding, - - - - 0 0 3

Fifth year, Clover.

Sixth year, Wheat.

Ploughing and sowing, - - - - - - 0 6 6
Weeding, - - - - 0 0 3

£.7 17 6
Balance in favour }
of the new system } 0 8 0

£.8 5 6

This calculation is made upon one acre of land from the old mode of fallowing once in every three years, or two crops and a fallow, which the *old* farmers call *not running* the land. With thofe I vary very much, as will be fhewn more fully in Section XLV.

The expences of the new mode are lefs by eight fhillings than thofe of the old in the firft fix years; and will fomewhat decreafe in the next fix years, except in manure, which will be more, as in my mode the refervoir and five crops of ftraw will produce nearly double the quantity. My manure is all raifed from the produce of the land it is laid on : but, to make his twelve loads, the *old* farmer robs the meadow or any piece of frefh land he is allowed to plough up. This is the principal caufe why fo many tenants are reftricted from ploughing old fwards ; as they do not carry back the manure to its proper place.

In all my calculations, I fuppofe that two loads of manure can be made from every acre of ftraw, if the crop be a good one. Therefore by the old fyftem (admitting the crop to be a good one, which frequently is not the cafe) there would be only eight loads of manure raifed in fix years, and by the new, ten loads, even without the affiftance of the refervoir. But in

the

the fecond fix years, if my plan be followed, I expect to have fourteen loads.

In making the above ftatement I have followed the ufual mode of calculations upon agriculture, by charging the manure as an expence; which, however, is very wrong, when it is not purchafed, but produced from the land.

SECTION IX.

Wheat-Crop through all the ftages, Drill-Hufbandry or Broad-Caft, Reaping, Thrafhing, cutting Straw for Chaff, &c.

TO fow wheat by the drill, fix pecks of feed are thought fufficient for one acre : but I fay, ten pecks ; for broad-caft, twelve. Two men with one horfe will drill with Cook's machine eight acres in one day. By broad-caft, one man will fow twelve.

To prevent the fmut in wheat, diffolve falt in water till an egg fwims in it : put your feed-wheat into the brine, and feparate the light grains that fwim at the top from thofe which fink. Some let it remain twenty-four hours in the brine : this I difapprove of, as it can produce no good, and bad confequences may enfue. When you have taken the wheat out

of

of the falt and water, fprinkle it over with chamberlie, or with water in which arfenic has been
boiled (one pound to eight gallons of water ;)
then throw on dry lime to make it fpread, and to
prevent the birds, which do not like the lime,
from eating it. Oats and barley may be prepared in the fame manner as wheat. The arfenic-water or chamberlie penetrates into the
infected or damaged grain, deftroys the vege-
tative power, and caufes it to rot in the ground;
by which means more room is left for the found
to grow. The operation with the chamberlie
or arfenic-water is dangerous; and often almoft
the whole crop is fpoiled by it. This will appear from the following accident that happened to me : the chamberlie, being taken from
the bottom of the tub where it was kept, and
confequently ftronger, killed the feed-wheat.
I had fteeped the wheat in falt and water over
night, as is our ufual way, and then fprinkled
it with chamberlie and lime. The time of
fowing was from eight o'clock in the morning
to four o'clock in the afternoon. The wheat
that was fown at eight in the morning, fprung
up the fame as that fown on the preceding day;
but kept declining, and became thinner and
thinner, until at laft fcarcely a tenth part grew.

A

A small part of the field which had been left unsown, was finished the next day; though in the night there fell much rain, and I had then an aversion to sowing any thing in wet weather. Being called from home for some time, my first pursuit, on returning, was to look how the wheat came up. To my great astonishment, that sown in the latter part of the first day looked very ill; I therefore enquired into the cause; and having great numbers of pigeons, I suspected they must have eaten it. I consequently returned to the field, and on searching into the mould, found thousands of the grain rotting. The wheat being all of one quality, and all prepared alike, I was more than ever puzzled. Knowing, however, there must be a cause, I reconsidered the whole; and at last I remembered the rainy night. The tub which had the chamberlie in it was uncovered, the rain had fallen into it, and had lowered the strength of the chamberlie; and consequently the wheat that was sown the last day was by far the best in the field. This circumstance had prevented me from ascribing the bad state of the wheat, to the chamberlie. But the chamberlie had certainly injured it, so that the part sown before the men went to dinner,

and that part sown after dinner, might be dis-
tinguished to an inch. Had the wheat remained unsown two hours longer, the chamberlie
would probably have killed it all. The part
sown after the rain was the best crop at reaping. I have since tried twenty experiments by
sowing in rain, or when land is wet; and I
always found it answer in the autumn. In
spring the practice is improper, as there is danger of the land's setting.

Shearing or reaping with the sickle is most
generally practised in respect to wheat when fit
to cut; but in some parts they *mow* it—a method I much disapprove of. Although reaping
costs double the price of mowing, the difference is much more than made up by the great
saving of grain, and by the goodness of the
straw for the purpose of cutting into chaff;
for by shearing you have only the fine part of
the straw, and it requires less carrying, and less
room in the barn or stack; and the stubble
serves for litter. If shorn, the best method of
securing wheat in the field for harvest, is to
set up ten sheaves against each other, and hood
or cap them. Hooding or capping will prevent the pigeons doing damage, and, by being
a good guard against rain, give an opportunity

to

to the corn of ftanding a fufficient time in the ftook to be ready for the barn.

Thrafhing is moft profitably performed by the machine, as will be explained in the following fection.

It is needlefs to fay any thing here of chopping of ftraw; as the operation is fo fimple and generally known, and frequently fpoken of in the courfe of the Work.

SECTION X.

Ufe of the Thrafhing-Machine.

BY thrafhing with the machine, little corn will be left in the ftraw. I do not mean to defcribe the machine minutely : the inventor is ready to give particulars to thofe who choofe to apply to him. It is fufficient for me to fay, that by the operation of this machine the corn is to a certainty freed from the ftraw and all extraneous matter. Thrafhing with the flail is uncertain at the beft, even fuppofing the thrafher difpofed to do his work well ; for he may beat a long time and not meet with every head of corn, which with the machine it is fcarcely poffible to mifs. The grain wafted by the ufe of the flail is beyond belief. One circum-

ftance

stance struck me forcibly as to the waste of wheat by bad thrashing. I had the curiosity, when in London (it was at the time her Royal Highness the Princess of Wales lay in), to look at the Prince's horses : some straw was then drawing into the stables, which I observed to be very slovenly thrashed. The court, or stable yard, was at the time covered with straw, on account of the Princess's situation : this of course was much beat by carriages ; and when the litter was taken up, the ground was strewn with corn. I am of opinion, the corn lost by thrashing with the flail is more than would pay for thrashing it all over the kingdom by the machine.

The only plausible objection to the thrashing machine I ever heard, is the expence attending the making and using it. But, the first expence will be counterbalanced by the saving in the erection of barns ; as one of a moderate size will be sufficient, where it is now necessary to build two or three of great extent. And those who object to the expence of working it know nothing of the matter. Experiments have been made upon what has been left by the flail, as well thrashed as men could do it : and on having it done over again by the ma-

chine

chine worked by one horfe, it has been found
to pay well for the trouble.

Every machine muft be worked by fome
power ; and whether the power is applied by
by means of living animals, by fire, wind, or
water, the effect will be the fame. The ufe of
water is attended with the leaft expence ; but
it is confined to particular fituations. Wind
is uncertain, even to a proverb. Fire, in countries where coal is cheap, may be applied to
great advantage ; fteam-engines being now
improved to a degree of perfection that heretofore they were thought impoffible of attaining.
They are dangerous, however, where ftraw is
concerned. But the power moft generally
ufed to put the thrafhing-machine in motion,
is that of living animals. A farmer intending
to erect one of thefe machines, will no doubt
proportion it to the fize of his farm, and to the
quantity of corn he means to thrafh ; though,
indeed, the power may be applied to many
other ufes. The dimenfions of this machine
may be fuch as to work with one horfe only ;
or it may be large enough to work with half a
dozen, where the farm is very extenfive, and
expedition is neceffary.

The

The machine will require five pair of hands to work it. But let not the farmer be alarmed at the number of hands mentioned; for one woman and four children will eafily work one upon a middling fcale.

The method is as follows : One takes the fheaf from the mow; another unties, fpreads, and lays it on a place proper for the third perfon, whofe bufinefs it is to feed the machine. This third perfon muft be a fteady one. A fourth takes away the ftraw. Fifthly, a boy to drive the horfe : but when the horfe becomes ufed to his work, a driver will be unneceffary. Be the fize of the farm more or lefs, there are almoft always horfes to be fpared for work of this kind, which may be fo contrived as to be done at a leifure time. But fuppofing the farm fo large as to employ a machine worked with *five* horfes ; it is highly probable that on fuch a farm there may be brood-mares, kept folely for the purpofe of breeding : it would be good economy to ufe fuch mares when the foals are taken from them, which is ufually done in the thrafhing-feafon. Such a practice would encourage the breeding of horfes ; and the mares fo ufed would raife their foals well, and lofe no time.

But

But the farmer is not confined to the ufe of horfes ; the employing oxen, or young growing fteers, would be profitable ; as in that cafe they would earn their meat. It is no doubt plea-fant to the farmer to derive a reafonable profit from all the animals he keeps; which might be the cafe here.

It is a miftaken notion to fuppofe that the ufe of this machine will decreafe the demand for labour. On the contrary, it will afford employment for children, who, unlefs they are placed in the neighbourhood of manufacturing towns, confume their youth in idlenefs, and contract a habit of pilfering ; beginning per-haps with hedge-breaking, and progreffively proceeding to crimes of a capital nature. An honeft man, fond of work, and inured to induf-try, will always meet with encouragement.

SECTION XI.

Different Sorts of Grain proper for different Soils.

WHEAT will grow upon almoft any foil, with proper care and management ; but it profpers beft upon a clay, loam, or wharp.

Barley

Barley delights in fandy or gravelly foils, or lime-ftone; yet, if a clay foil be well managed, it will produce the beft barley for the purpofe of making malt; for when properly manufactured, malt made from barley that has grown on clay-land is found to be more abundant in that faccharine juice in which confifts its value for the brewer. Barley will not thrive on moor-land, or peat-earth; nor does it like a low and wet fituation.

Oats will grow upon any foil, but bear the heavieft and fineft crops upon gravel or fand. Fen-lands will produce abundant crops of oats, as will in general all low land, if of a good quality. Lime-ftone land very feldom produces large crops of oats; neither is a ftiff clay favourable to the propagation of this grain.

Beans fucceed beft on a clay foil, loam, or wharp. With manure and proper management they will grow on any foil; but on few fo well as on clay.

Peas will grow and profper on almoft any foil. They will produce abundantly, and with lefs manure than any grain I ever made trial of.

Tares will thrive well on all foils; they grow fpontaneoufly on poor foils of a dry nature.

Garden-peas

Garden-peas I have lately found to bear the winter much better than the field-pea, with the same treatment. But they all require a little manure. Four loads per acre will produce upon a middling soil a good crop.

SECTION XII.

Turnip-Culture in all the different Stages ; with the great Advantage of the Drill.

TO raife turnip-feed in the beft manner, you muft pull up, from the field where they ftood all winter, fome turnips of the moft approved forts (I prefer the white-top, or the ftone-turnip), and plant them in a fmall fpot of ground— a dozen will produce plenty of feed. Preferve that feed, and fow it in fome convenient place, to raife feed for your whole crop the next year. Put them in drills, and do not hoe them ; but draw them out by hand, leaving fuch plants as take the lead. When they have appled or turned, carefully pull out every improper turnip. By following the above method, your feed will be more vigorous, will vegetate with lefs moifture, and produce ftronger and hardier plants. It is ufual at prefent to tranfplant a large quantity of turnips to raife feed for the whole crop, which practice is more expenfive and very injurious ; for, by pulling the turnip and planting it again, you deftroy the tap-root, and weaken the turnip's ftrength and vigour, fo that the feed from it muft be of an inferior quality.

By drilling the turnips it is highly probable every plant will grow to perfection, if the manure be properly depofited ; and, by making the drills, a hollow place is left, which will both attract and retain moifture ; and likewife fhade the plants from the heat of the fun, and thus deprive the fly, which is fo dangerous an enemy to the turnip, in fome meafure of her favourite fituation. Drilling likewife empowers the farmer to fow the feed much thicker ; and it is much lefs liable to be all devoured by the fly when fo fown, than when fuperficially fcattered by the broad-caft. By the latter method the feed is fprinkled unequally ; and by adventitious circumftances (fuch as a puff of wind, or part of the feed falling on a hard clod higher than the reft of the land, and rebounding to a diftance from the fpot it was intended to to be depofited upon) it is poffible a large fpace

may

may be left nearly void, or perhaps with only a plant or two. Now it too often happens that the mifchievous fly attacks the very plants fo thinly fown, and by deftroying them leaves a large fpace of ground uncovered. It is certainly a moft difficult tafk regularly to cover the land by the broad-caft : on the contrary, by the drill-method the feed will all fall into the hollow part, and the mould (efpecially if harrowed with the bufh-harrow) will be fo finely pulverifed, as to afford immediate nourifhment to it ; by which means the plants will get quickly forward. And when they are ready for hoeing, it will not require fo expert a hand to divide them ; and it will be eafier to choofe the mafter plant, which is of great importance in a crop of any kind. When they are planted in rows, any boy, girl, or woman, may do the bufinefs effectually ; and as this operation is performed at a feafon of the year when men have generally full employment in other branches of hufbandry, it is convenient to the farmer that women or children may anfwer his purpofe, and that at a cheaper rate than taking men from more important concerns.

After

After the turnip has acquired fufficient strength to bear ploughing the earth from the plants, it muft be done without delay. The firft ploughing will add fufficient earth to the plant according to the then fize. The turnips may be made to grow to what fize the farmer choofes (according to the nature of his foil) by only leaving them from fix to twelve inches afunder in the rows : and he may at any time add earth fufficient to prevent their rotting by froft in winter.

This often occafions great lofs : but the farmer may eafily guard againft it, by covering them properly with mould ; for he may plough as often as he choofes, and at his leifure, after the turnips are up ; and in the rows he may pluck up the weeds any time before they get into feed. Turnips fown as above directed ftand moift in fummer and dry in winter.

The fecuring a crop by laying from *four* to *fix* loads per acre of manure, as heretofore defcribed, inftead of *twelve*, is too great an advantage to be neglected.

In eating turnips off with fheep, great lofs is frequently fuftained from want of proper management ; but more particularly in the broad-
caft,

caft, where the cuftom is to give fheep a large fold of turnips. Perhaps froft comes on immediately, and continues fome days ; a fall of fnow probably fucceeds : in fuch cafe, even the moft obftinate advocate for the old method certainly muft allow the drill to be far preferable ; as it would be eafy to have fheep-pens or turnip-trays made and fet in fuch a manner as to form a kind of trough, moveable of courfe. The bar or tray muft be fet near the far fide of the row of turnips ; and a board, from ten to twelve inches broad, with two or three ftakes (longer or fhorter according to the depth of the foil) nailed to it, muft be fixed on the fide where the fheep are to eat ; for the narrower the fpace the turnips are enclofed in, the better. It may poffibly be feared left the fheep fhould get in amongft the turnips fenced off. I fay, no. For, fuppofing the turnips to take up a regular fpace of twelve inches, the trough may be made not much more than a foot wide at bottom, floping upward : and the tray or bar may incline towards the fheep and hang over the trough, or part where the turnips are, and prevent them from getting into it.

By

By this means sheep might have their food quite clean; and by setting off only the quantity necessary for the day, they would eat their portion with avidity, and not dung upon it, and spoil more than they eat. Every animal has a natural antipathy to its own excrement: can we then suppose such clean feeders as sheep an exception to the general rule? Even their lying down upon their food gives these delicate creatures disgust; and they have so great an aversion for what they have lain upon, that, unless impelled by hunger, they will not meddle with it. Will any farmer indiscriminately use certain utensils of his bed-chamber for the purposes to which those of his kitchen are generally applied?

The opulent farmer, who may chance to read this, will probably exclaim: " This method may suit a man who has a small flock; but what am I to do with thousands and tens of thousands of sheep?" I answer: Examine the difference in expence, you will find my method cheaper than driving your thousands or tens of thousands from ten to fifty miles from home. For, besides the loss of manure, and the waste of turnip, you will not be able to see them, per-

haps,

haps, above once in a month ; and though your ſhepherd be a careful fellow, the flock will be diminiſhed by diſaſters which they would not have been liable to under the eye of the maſter. By keeping the ſheep at home, in the manner before deſcribed, they will tread the ground regularly, and conſiderably enrich the farm by depoſiting their manure where it ought to be ; and, on the *loweſt* calculation, three ſheep may be kept this way to two by the old method—perhaps even double the number : and by obſerving the regularity recommended above, they will fatten much ſooner than by the old ſyſtem.

It is well underſtood in feeding cattle, horſes, pigs, &c. that if you lay a redundancy of food before them, they will not, in many inſtances, feed ſo well : they eat juſt ſufficient to ſatisfy nature, and waſte the reſt.

If the ſheep were driven into ſtraw-folds, they might breakfaſt on ſtraw, which would cauſe them to retain the turnips longer in their ſto-machs, and thus to fatten ſooner. Meanwhile the ſhepherd and boy might be moving the fold a row farther; or, if found more convenient, they might move the ſheep early in the evening

to

to the ftraw-fold, and at that time fhift the pen. Where there are both feeding fheep and ftock fheep, it would be advifable to give the feeding fheep rather more than fufficient for the day, and the next day to turn the ftock fheep into the fold to eat up what the others had left. By this method, a man may foon judge what length of turnips to give to the fheep, fo as to commit little or no wafte.

The advantage of my method will appear from the following calculation: Suppofe two hundred fheep to employ one man and one boy every day. I agree, the boy might be fuperfluous in the old way; but allow one fhilling per day for him. The fame quantity of turnips I eftimate to keep three fheep where only two were kept before. Three hundred fheep will then be kept where only two hundred were kept. Reckoning the profit on one hundred fheep at two-pence weekly per head, it will amount to 16s. 8d. per week; and deducting from it the extra charge of feven fhillings for the boy, there remains a clear profit of 9s. 8d. per week. If the flock is larger, the profit will increafe in proportion; as a man and boy can manage four hundred fheep. Two hundred

are

are fufficient to be fed together: but if four hundred were equally divided, a man and boy could manage both flocks.

But I am of opinion, that even *two* fheep may be kept by my method for *one* in the old way. If fo, the money would be 1*l.* 13*s.* 4*d* per week, which in twenty weeks would amount to 33*l.* 6*s.* 8*d.* which fum would more than clear the expences of the boy, and of the extraordinary pen the firft feafon.

Where cattle are to be fed on turnips, they may be treated in the fame manner as fheep, provided the land be dry.

Having fo plainly demonftrated the fuperiority of turnip-culture by the drill, it would be fuperfluous to fay more of the broad caft. The latter method will, I hope, be exploded by every farmer who can prevail upon himfelf to give the former a fair trial. To render what is above recommended more eafy and no lefs profitable, it may be proper to plant, along with the turnips, in the middle of the field, a proper fpace (proportioned to the fize of your flock) with potatoes, which might be taken up at the proper feafon; and the vacant ground would ferve for the fheep to pafs to and fro to eat their food.

To preserve the potatoes from frost, make them into what we call a *pie:* a term well understood in Yorkshire; but perhaps not very intelligible in other parts of the Island. For the manner of making such a *pie,* see Section XVII.

Potatoes might be given to the sheep in frosty weather, when it would be difficult to move the trays or pens. They might be given in the space where the turnips had been. If you have more potatoes than necessary for the sheep, you may feed milch-cows with them; as milk and butter are far better from potatoe-food than turnips. In fact, potatoes are excellent food for cattle of all kinds.

SECTION XIII.

Best Method of Seeding Land; Quantity necessary and proper Sort for every Soil.

THE best method of sowing seeds, if with barley or any spring crop, is to sow them after the corn is in, and the ground is harrowed to a fine mould. After sowing them, it is a good method immediately to bush-harrow, and to roll the earth, for from want of such precaution many of them fail of producing the expected

pected crop; as, not being fufficiently fixed in the earth, they are liable to be over-fcorched by the fun, or deftroyed by birds or otherwife. This rolling and bufh-harrowing not only prevents, but likewife affifts in reducing the mould to a more equal degree of finenefs and fmoothnefs.

On land of any kind, intended for pafture, my practice is to fow four bufhels of rye-grafs, ten pounds of trefoil, and ten pounds of white clover, per acre. If the land is intended to be mown, and it is required to have rye-grafs, one or two pecks of that feed is fufficient, with ten pounds of red clover, and fix pounds of trefoil, per acre.

If the rye-grafs is omitted, but the crop intended for mowing; fourteen pounds of red clover, with fix of trefoil, per acre, will be neceffary.

If feeds are fown in fpring, upon land fown with wheat the preceding autumn, the following method will beft cover them. Harrow the land, if it will bear it, and roll it immediately after, If the wheat is to be eaten with fheep, fow the feeds; then lay on fuch a number of fheep as will tread the land fufficiently within two or three days. A large flock will

eat

eat the wheat within that time, and tread the feeds into the earth far better than if you put in half the quantity of sheep, and let that half remain double the time; for they eat the weakest wheat first, and let the strong alone: therefore the greater the number of sheep the better. When they are taken out, bush-harrow and roll immediately.

Of saintfoin sow not less than five bushels, and from that to eight bushels, per acre, though four bushels is the usual quantity: for as saintfoin is intended to be mown for a number of years, the difference in the expence of the seed, at first sowing, is trifling, when it is considered, that by sowing the quantity recommended you may get every year one ton of hay more per acre, than by sowing four bushels only. I never knew an instance of a crop of saintfoin, or any other grafs, being injured by sowing the seed thick.

Saintfoin should be sown in a clean fallow, upon a spring crop, and harrowed in and rolled immediately. Almost any sort of soil that has a rocky bottom, or a white clay, is proper for it; but it will not thrive well except upon land with a firm bottom. Saintfoin certainly finds

food

food in ftone, as in the foil it is partial to there
can be little or no food in the furface, efpecially for fuch a number of years. I have been
told that where ftone-quarries have been made
after faintfoin has grown on the land, the roots
have been found to ftrike feveral feet down into
the rock. This is a profitable herb, far exceeding any yet propagated on poor land: no other
is fo beneficial to the farmer, according to the
value of the land it is fown upon; but great
care muft be taken, if manure be laid upon it,
that fuch manure be as clear from grafs-feeds
of different kinds as poffible; for faintfoin is
very liable to be injured by adventitious feeds
getting amongft it. Pigeons' dung, rape-duft,
malt-combs, foot, or almoft any *hand-manure*,
are proper. Saintfoin, if properly fown, and
on fuitable land, will bear good crops from ten
to fourteen years; may be eaten with fheep for
three years afterwards, and will maintain three
times more ftock than the produce of the land
in the natural ftate. I have known it mown
for fourteen years. The firft year there will
always be a thin crop; but the fucceeding ten
years it has yielded upwards of two tons per
acre, on land which at this time is not worth
more

more than five shillings per acre for any other
use. Saintfoin ought always to be preserved
for mowing. The method of treating it is as
follows:—If sown in the spring with barley;
when the barley is mown, the stubble must be
left high. It would be much better if the barley were shorn, as the stubble would then afford
shelter for the plant during winter. Rake the
stubble off in the spring; but put no stock
upon it from the time of harvesting the barley
to the time of mowing the first crop, which, as
I said before, will not be abundant. In the
month of September there will be after-grass,
which may be depastured by sheep and beasts,
but not by horses. Sheep must not be kept
on it after the frost sets in; for, by eating too
near the root, at the latter end of the year they
will do the plant much injury. This caution
is, therefore, absolutely necessary.

No stock must be put upon this grass in the
spring; and it will be ready to mow early in
summer, most probably in the beginning of
June. It must not be suffered to grow too
long before it is mown, or many bad consequences may ensue; for the root is thereby
exhausted, and the duration of the plant much
short-

shortened. If full blown, the spirituous and nourishing juices are spent and lost, the sap is impoverished, and the hay destitute of that richness which it possesses when cut early. But, above all, it should be mown before any of the flowers begin to decay. It is impossible to get this kind of hay over-green; but care must be taken that it be well dried. Very moderate care will suffice for that purpose, as from the stalkiness of the plant the air has a freedom of circulation when the hay is in small cocks. But if it be laid up rather green, it will be adviseable to have a chimney or vent-hole, from the bottom to the top of the rick, through which the superfluous moisture may exhale; and when the heating is over, the rick must be thatched. All ricks of this hay perfectly dried ought to be thatched with as much expedition as possible after they are made. That which is put into the rick perfectly dried, will cut out of a green colour; but that which has been laid up over-moist, will be liable to heat much, and consequently become brown.

Saintfoin (so much esteemed in France, that our Gallic neighbours have canonized it by adding the epithet *holy*) is for horses undoubtedly the best hay hitherto known. Many

farmers

farmers keep them the whole winter upon it without much corn, and the horfes are fat and fine as hunters. Poft-horfes thrive well upon it, and, next to corn, nothing will keep them in fuch good heart. It is excellent for fheep, but not proper for cows. If the crop has been fuffered to remain until it was ripe, and the hay be thrafhed for feed, it is ftill fit for horfes, and may be cut into chaff, and will give as much nourifh-ment as treble the quantity of chaff from ftraw. If the farmer has a redundancy of feeds after thrafhing, they may with great advantage be given to horfes in lieu of corn, in the propor-tion of *three* to *four*.

By mowing this grafs early in the fummer, the eddifh, or after-grafs, will fpring imme-diately, and be foon fit to be depaftured; and the ftock may be taken out fooner in the autumn. It has been objected, that faintfoin is a great impoverifher of land; but I requeft thofe who have adopted fuch an opinion upon truft, to keep a debtor and creditor account: for I infift that no plant in ufe will improve land fo quickly, with fo great a profit, at fuch a fmall expence. If we confider, that two tons of hay will make three loads of excellent ma-nure; allowing one load of ftraw to litter the

horfes,

horfes, there will remain two loads of manure
yearly to the account of the faintfoin, for each
acre. The poor land upon which this hay is
grown would not produce one ton of hay from
natural grafs in ten years; but by being fown
with faintfoin it is capable of raifing within
that period twenty loads of manure of an excellent quality. In the natural ftate of the
land, it would not raife more than one load of
manure in ten years, and even that of fuch
a quality as to be worth little or nothing.
When faintfoin is exhaufted and ploughed
up; from the faintfoin ley the firft crop ought
to be wheat dibbled, or peas. If you plough
early in the winter to let the froft act upon the
land; and in the fpring drill, and manure with
four loads per acre of its own manure, and
fow the peas as directed in fection XLV,
a productive crop would follow. We have
now, for the ten years, fixteen loads of manure
remaining on hand for each acre. The next
winter a fallow for turnips. Debit for fix loads
more manure per acre for a crop of turnips,
drilled and eaten off with fheep, which would
put the land in a proper ftate for barley and
clover. We can then afford to manure the

young clover in the autumn, with the remaining ten loads; but five loads made into compost would be fufficient, and bring a very luxuriant crop; and there being fo much manure in the land, we may expect good wheat. After this we fhall have another turnip fallow; and having lent to the farm in general a crop of pea-ftraw, a crop of barley-ftraw, a crop of clover, and a crop of wheat-ftraw, all this ftuff may raife ten loads of manure. We therefore call for fix loads for each acre again, and have another turnip crop, then barley and grafs-feeds for fheep, if required. Now we have four loads of manure (or nine, if the compoft be ufed in the clover crop) owing to every acre of land; we have received no intereft for the ufe of the ten crops of faintfoin manure, nor of the peas, barley, clover or wheat; the intereft of fuch manure being lent during that time. If we fay, four loads per acre ought to be paid in lieu of intereft, it will be much below the quantity: but we will eftimate it at only four loads, and we fhall then have eight loads (or thirteen) to lay on our young grafs-feeds, which are to be depaftured by fheep for two years and then ploughed up again, &c.

After

After this fair ftatement, who fhall fay faint-foin is detrimental to land ? But, as a further elucidation, we will fuppofe a gentleman to grant his tenant a leafe for twenty-one years, with free liberty to follow the method here laid down ; and another gentleman to retain the fame quantity of land in the natural ftate, for the like term of twenty-one years. We allow frefh land to bring more luxuriant crops than old going land ; but I dare fay every one will allow the land that has been fown with faint-foin, which is now ready to enter upon in frefh feeds with eight loads of manure upon it per acre, will at leaft feed ten ewes and lambs on each acre for two months, four fheep for the reft of the fummer, and two from that time until Chriftmas.

Now on the other hand, what will the land of the fame quality do in the natural ftate ? During the twenty-one years it has not kept any thing in the winter feafons, and not more than a fheep per acre in fummer.

The fuperior advantages arifing from a rota-tion of faintfoin, and other crops for twenty-one years will appear clearly from the follow-ing ftatements,

Account

Account of Expences and Profit on an Acre of Land, sown with Saintfoin and other Crops, according to my Method.

Dr. to EXPENCES.	Cr. by PRODUCE.
	£. s. d.
1st Year, TURNIPS.	By turnips 2 12 6
£. s. d.	
To paring and burn-	
ing 1 1 0	
To ploughing and	
feed 0 6 0	
To hoeing 0 5 0	
To rent 0 5 0	
To affeffment 0 5 0	
*£.*2 2 0	*£.*2 12 6
2d Year, BARLEY.	By three quarters of
To ploughing and	barley, at 25s. per
fowing 0 6 0	quarter 3 15 0
To feed, three bufh. 0 10 0	
To faintfoin feed 2 10 0	
To rent and affeffment 0 10 0	
*£.*3 16 0	*£.*3 15 0
3d Year, SAINTFOIN.	
To rent and affeffment 0 10 0	By one ton faintfoin
To mowing, &c. 0 5 6	hay 4 0 0
*£.*0 15 6	*£.*4 0 0
4th Year, SAINTFOIN.	
The expence will be	By two ton of faint-
the fame fo long	foin hay 8 0 0
as the field is in	By eddifh 0 10 0
faintfoin 0 15 6	
*£.*0 15 6	*£.*8 10 0
*£.*7 9 0	*£.*18 17 6

Dr. to EXPENCE.	Cr. by PRODUCE.
Brt. over £.7 9 0	Brt. over £.18 17-6
5th, 6th, 7th, 8th, 9th, 10th, 11th, 12th, 13th, 14th, which is ten years expences.	
£. s. d.	£. s. d.
Rents, affeffments, &c. 15s. 6d. per year 7 15 0	By ten years hay and eddifh, at £.8 10s. per year 85 0 0
£.7 15 0	£.85 0 0
15th, 16th, 17th, Depaftured with SHEEP.	
Rent and affeffment for three years 1 10 0	By one ewe and lamb per acre, for three years 3 0 0
£.1 10 0	£.3 0 0
18th Year, PEAS in Drills, or WHEAT dibbled.	
To ploughing and harrowing 0 7 6	By three quarters of peas 6 0 0
To four loads of manure, leading, &c. 0 3 6	By ftraw 1 0 0
To feed peas, one fack 1 3 0	
To rent and affeffment 0 10 0	
To reaping and thrafhing 0 5 0	
£.2 6 0	£.7 0 0
£.19 0 0	£.113 17 6

Dr. to EXPENCE.	Cr. by PRODUCE.
Brt. over £.19 0 0	Bt. over £.113 17 6

19th Year, TURNIPS.

	£. s. d.		£. s. d.
To two ploughings and harrowing	0 15 0	By turnips	3 0 0
To drilling	0 2 6		
To manure, leading six loads	0 4 6		
To sowing seed, and harrowing	0 1 0		
To hoeing	0 3 0		
To three ploughings	0 4 6		
To rent and assessments	0 10 0		
£.2 0 6		**£.3 0 0**	

20th Year, BARLEY.

To ploughing and harrowing	0 6 6	By barley, four quarters, at 25s. per quarter	5 0 0
To one sack of barley	0 12 6		
To one quarter of rye-grass, and ten pounds of white clover and ten pounds of trefoil	2 10 0		
£.3 9 0		**£.5 0 0**	

21st Year, in SEEDS.

To rent and assessment	0 10 0	By profit on sheep	4 0 0
£.0 10 0		**£.4 0 0**	
		£.125 17 6	
£.24 19 6			
Profit in 21 years £.100 18 0			
£.125 17 6			

Account of Expences and Profit on an Acre of Land, left in its natural State.

Dr. to EXPENCE.	Cr. by PRODUCE.
£. s. d.	£. s. d.
To rent and affeff- ments for twenty- one years 10 10 0 To profit in twenty- one years 5 5 0	By twenty-one years herbage, one ewe and lamb, on an acre in the summer, and nothing in the winter 15 15 0
£.15 15 0	£.15 15 0

There is then a clear profit of £.100 18s. upon one acre by my method of cropping, for twenty-one years. I do not think it is poffible to apply this fort of land to a better purpofe, when a farm can fpare a proper quantity of it for that ufe. In the natural ftate it has paid £.5 5s. in twenty-one years, which is juft 5s. per acre, and as much as can be expected.

Red clover ought not to be fown but where the land is intended to lie for only one year. It is, in my opinion, the beft preparation for wheat, when the ground it is fown upon is per-fectly clean; but by no means fo, when the land is foul and full of couch-grafs, &c. The feed fhould be fown with the fpring crop of

barley

barley or oats. The clover crop lies eighteen months, after which only one ploughing will be requifite before the field be fown with wheat. The wheat will be about ten months on the ground; and it will be two months after the crop is reaped, before it be fallowed for turnips, &c; which together makes a period of thirty months for one ploughing. By letting the clover crop lie 18 months, the couch-grafs gets a very ftrong root; and, when the land is ploughed for wheat, and the foil lightened, that pernicious weed will fpread rapidly around. Therefore all poffible care fhould be taken to clean the field thoroughly, before it is fown with turnips, and made ready for barley and clover; for, if you neglect the opportunity of doing it at that time, you will not have another before April three years after.

Red clover is properly a native of a clay foil; but will fucceed upon almoft any, in proportion to the goodnefs of the land. It is improper to be fown with grafs-feeds, when intended for pafture or meadow; for, as it has a root not only very large, but likewife very broad at the bottom; and as it tillers very much, it muft of courfe obftruct their growth. Trefoil is very

proper

proper to be fown with red-clover ; as trefoil grows with a fmall vine-like fibre, which runs up with the clover fomething like rodded peas. By that means, the crop, from the fupport it receives from the clover, becomes fuller and more weighty, and the hay much better than it poffibly could be without fuch affiftance.

Clover may be depaftured in the autumn by fheep; and even in fpring, if abfolute neceffity fhould require it ; but it is better, if poffible, not to admit them to it at that feafon. The beft crop of clover I ever had was from letting turnip-fheep run at leifure upon a field of it, for about four months in the winter. It confifted of about twelve acres, fituated at the corner of a fixty acres' walk : and being fhort of fencing, and the reft of my clover very good, I thought I would run the rifk of fpoiling the twelve acres. Three hundred fheep ran upon it until the twentieth of February. They were then moved from it, and at the time they were ta-ken away, you could not, at a few yards diftance difcover the piece to have been clover—in fome places, not even if you walked over it. But when it was mown, it turned out, as obferved above, the moft abundant crop I had ever ob-

VOL. I. K tained.

tained. I do think, there were two tons and a half per acre. On the above experiment I have to remark, that the sheep, by running and lying on the clover, and there depositing their excrement, deprived the barley land of its manure; and that it furnishes a strong proof of what manure is capable of performing; for, had those twelve acres been eaten by only as many sheep as they would have kept, the crop in all probability had been spoiled.

When clover is to be followed by wheat, it is better to mow it twice in one summer; as mowing will not only clear the land of weeds, but will render it more mellow, and pulverise it for the reception of the wheat. For, if the ground were at that season of the year, after the first mowing, totally covered with a stack of straw, it would produce better wheat. I once had a proof of this, by stacking some woodkids or faggots upon a part of the land where clover had been mown once. The stack remained until the time of sowing wheat; and on the spot where it stood was by far the best wheat in the field.

I have had many instances of clover being better for twice mowing. I have tried experiments,

ments, by eating one part with sheep all the summer, cropping or mowing a part, fencing another part, and eating with sheep after mowing. Another I mowed once, and then attempted to get feed from the after-crop. The season setting in wet, I mowed and took it off for manure into the fold-yard. I then ploughed the land, and sowed it the next day; and that part of the field produced by far the best crop of wheat, in respect both to quantity and goodness of grain. I have ploughed the second crop of clover in; but I never found any benefit from that.

When you intend the red clover for hay, you must watch very closely in respect to the time of cutting; for, shoud you mow it too soon, and the weather turn out wet, the crop would quickly receive damage, and be a long time getting ready for stacking. If on the contrary you let it stand too long, until the leaf, which is the best part of the clover, begins to fall, it makes the stalks stumpy, and you suffer great loss by the dropping of the leaf, and by the waste of the most pleasant and nutritive part of the hay. It certainly is preferable to be rather too soon, than too late, in mowing. For,

though

though clover fhould be harvefted dry, it fhould be preferved green, fo as to admit of one fourth part of wheat-ftraw being added to and ftacked with it, by alternate layers of hay and ftraw. The confequence of this management will be, that, from the fweating of the clover in the ftack, the ftraw will imbibe the fubtil odoriferous effluvia of the plant, and be in fome degree impregnated with the oily vapour that exhales from the clover, which without fuch precaution would be diffipated and loft. When fuch hay and ftraw are cut together, they make better food than clover and ftraw cut feparately into chaff. For, from the quantity of oil this plant abounds with, and from the frothinefs of its nature, it is not advifable to give a horfe deftined to work hard too great a quantity, without an allay of one half ftraw, to cool him and affift in promoting a regular digeftion.

Great care muft be taken to put no more ftraw into the ftack than the clover will bear, fo as not to prevent the whole from taking a regular and neceffary heat. This method is attended with another advantage; you may ftack your clover without fear of danger from heating to excefs, many days fooner than you

otherwife

otherwife could have done. When I fpeak of
giving an *equal* quantity of ftraw with the clover to horfes, I do not mean that as much ftraw
as clover fhould be put in the ftack ; for that
would entirely prevent it from heating. As
clover is not much fafer in the cock than in the
fwathe, the method I recommend will be
found ufeful ; for, as foon as the clover is fit
to cock, you may ftack it, and by that means
often fave the crop, inftead of running the rifk
of many days' delay, by waiting to ftack it according to the old method.

I have found it beneficial to fow rye-grafs
with clover, by way of making it hardier to
harveft; but rye-grafs is an enemy to the following crop of wheat, and wheat-ftraw is more
beneficial when put in the ftack. Rye-grafs is
a fort of grafs I am very partial to : but no
doubt I fhall find many differ from me in opinion. However, I by experience know that
one acre fown for fheep with rye-grafs, white
clover and trefoil, will maintain a proportion
of three to two fheep more than with any other
kind of grafs, or mixture of graffes, I know of.
When I fay *of three to two*, I mean for twelve
months ; as rye-grafs is both the earlieft and

the

the lateſt. In the ſpring it cannot be eaten too early, if the animals can but live upon it; for, if it be ſuffered to ſpindle, it will be exhauſted before the ſpring, or beſt ſeaſon is over: on the contrary, if eaten cloſe, it will keep continually ſpringing, as cabbages ſprout after being cut; and the more it is eaten, the more it will grow.

At the time when the rye-graſs is ſo very luxuriant, the white clover is totally concealed in the ground, but the trefoil makes ſome ſmall appearance; and when the rye-graſs has done all that can be expected, the trefoil ſprings up and becomes food for the ſheep; after which the white clover ſucceeds, and in like manner ſupplies the ſheep or cattle. When the white clover is done, the rye-graſs again ſprings up, and continues growing all winter, if the weather prove tolerably open. At all events, it will grow if any graſs *can grow*.

If you intend it for meadow, and ſow one ſack upon an acre, it will be like throwing the feeds of the trefoil and white clover away; as rye-graſs, by ſpringing ſo early and by ſmothering the land, prevents the others from growing to any degree of perfection.

The

The feed of rye-grafs is rarely to be found pure. Much of what is fold is, in general, a mixture of fwine-grafs, couch, and feveral other noxious forts: and this is the reafon why this feed is fo generally difliked, and why rye-grafs is faid to fill land full of twitch or couch-grafs. But this is an erroneous opinion; for rye-grafs will no more produce twitch than it will produce wheat. Therefore, the farmer muft either have fown the feeds of twitch with the feeds of rye-grafs; or, at the time he prepared the land, muft have left the plants or feeds of twitch in the ground. The fact is, that great part of the feed fold for rye-grafs, is in reality chiefly that of twitch ; for this kind of feed is moft frequently raifed by the lower fort of farmers, who, not having money fufficient to purchafe ftock for the purpofe of eating the herbage, meadow it and let it ftand for feed, crops of which it will produce for many years. But, if there be any twitch when the rye-grafs is firft fown, the twitch, as being more luxuriant, will increafe the fafteft and in length of time get into fole poffeffion of the field. At prefent, there is very little land in England without twitch. I know no herb which

increafes

increases so rapidly, or which it is so difficult to destroy.

To enable the farmer to distinguish rye-grass, it will be necessary to describe the seed. Real rye-grass has seed something like rye, short and black-hearted, very full of flour and very heavy, as it will weigh from eight to nine stone per sack, reckoning fourteen pounds to the stone, and four bushels Winchester measure to the sack. The seed of couch-grass is longer and lighter, the root of the plant joints, and so do the branches, and it is so succulent that every joint will emit a root. There are a great many species of it. As this plant is so abundant, the earth no doubt is strongly impregnated with the seed, which renders the total eradication of it next to impossible. But yet, although it cannot be totally destroyed, it may by good management *be kept under*.

On my return from valuing an estate in the county of Lincoln, I passed over some land rented by a farmer, and there saw the most prolific crop of twitch I ever before had met with. I believe that had the roots been carefully collected, dried and stacked, they would have proved more abundant, and formed a much

larger

larger ftack than any quantity of hay that
could have been raifed from the fame piece of
land by the art and induftry of man. The roots,
in light foils, run in a moft aftonifhing manner,
much more than I thought poffible, until I faw
the above-mentioned field. I was told however, that it had been fown with what had been
called rye-grafs feed, and that the farmer had
likewife fold as fuch the feed produced from
it. No wonder twitch is fo common! I do
not fuppofe one fingle acre of rye-grafs in the
kingdom is to be found without it; becaufe fo
little care is taken in felecting the feed, in the
choice of which much knowledge and great
circumfpection are neceffary. Rye-grafs is a
very fine grafs with a fmall bufhy root, full of
fibres, but fhort; and, when the land is ploughed up and fown with corn, may be deftroyed
with as much eafe as clover. But as it feeds
every year, there will undoubtedly be much of
the feed fhed, which will appear in the enfuing
crops.

Rye-grafs is thought to impoverifh land;
but (allowing this to be true, which in many
cafes may be owing to the quantity of twitch
fown with it) the returns, and the great quan-

tity of stock maintained by it, fully compensate for what it takes from the land. It may not be so proper to sow wheat after rye-grass, as it is a sort of white crop like wheat, and requires the same kind of nourishment. It may be better followed by a crop of peas: but I prefer wheat dibbled.

Rye-grass, if mown for hay, should be cut when in blossom, and got in green. The hay made from it does not heat or sweat much, and is very good for horses, but not for sheep or cattle. If it is suffered to stand too long before it be cut, the seeds rob the plant of the juices, and leave it no better than wheat or rye-straw.

Clay land is most proper to raise the seed of rye-grass upon: as twitch-grass does not delight in, and may with more ease be cleared from, such soil, than from any other. I have known a strong clayey land laid down very full of the roots of twitch-grass; and, by the succeeding summer proving dry, and sheep treading the ground, and eating the grass bare, it has, when ploughed up, been nearly clear.

Rye-grass is not so proper to be sown for mowing, for it tillers very little, but readily

shoots

shoots up; and if depastured, it will branch
for a long time before it runs into feed. To
prevent this, you must crowd it with different
kinds of stock, such as sheep, beasts, and horses;
and if of different ages, they will be more likely to clear the land by eating the crop clean
off; for if it be suffered to run to feed, the
root becomes exhausted. If, in spite of the
stock you have put on, you find a disposition
in the grass to feed, increase the number of horses, which are the only animals that are fond
of it when feeding; and you may diminish
the number of sheep, for in that state of the
plant they derive but little nourishment from
it, as few leaves are then left upon the stem;
which is one reason for sowing trefoil and white
clover with it.

Trefoil is esteemed a bitter plant, and sheep
are thought not to be fond of it; but I must
own that nothing within the compass of my experience has led me to adopt this opinion.
Trefoil grows about a month earlier than
white-clover, and long before the rye-grass is
exhausted. It is improper to be sown alone,
except for the express purpose of raising feed.
There are no soils proper for trefoil but what
will

will produce rye-grafs and white-clover. Hay made from trefoil only is a pretty hay, but not very abundant in the produce. I am of opinion I could raife more trefoil on any given quantity of land, by fowing rye-grafs amongft it than without; for, as before obferved, trefoil, like the vine and pea, wants fupport from fome ftronger fubftance it may cling to. For this reafon it will alfo profper well with red-clover, around which its tendrils will twine like woodbines in a thorn hedge. I alfo do believe that the crop of clover will be very little lefs in quantity or weight from the trefoil growing amongft it.

The after-grafs of trefoil is worth very little; for which reafon fome people recommend it to be followed by wheat. But I can affert from continued experience, that land intended for wheat cannot poffibly be too much fmothered with crops of every fort.

White clover is thought to be an herb that fheep are very fond of: I believe they may; but I do not efteem it much. It is a tardy plant, and yields but a fmall quantity of hay in comparifon with many others. In quality it is of a fattening nature (which may partly

arife

arife from its fpringing fo late in the feafon);
but I never found it fuperior in any refpect to
red clover; nor do I think it near fo ufeful.
Red-clover, when made into hay, is excellent
food for all forts of animals. White-clover
grows only about two months with any degree
of vigour, and requires much warmth before it
fprings up. It will grow upon any foil; for
all foils contain its feed. The barren commons
near Buxton in Derbyfhire, when limed, will
produce fine white clover : and we are fure
that no feed has been fown upon it except by
the hand of Providence ; for it is well-known
that lime paffes through the fire before it is
ufed as manure, and confequently cannot contain feed of white-clover or of any other plant.
The uncultivated land in North-America
abounds with white-clover. The earth, indeed,
feems to have been impregnated with its feed
from the creation ; as any kind of land, when
manured, will produce it. From curiofity, I took
a dry clod of clay, pounded and fifted it, and
found white-clover feed. I then put the whole
of the pulverifed matter into a garden-pot, and
had the fatisfaction of feeing white-clover fpring
up. Almoft every herb delights more in one

kind

kind of foil than in another : but I believe white-clover to be the leaft partial of any. Few animals like the nap of white-clover : you fee it in every pafture remain until the feed is per-fectly ripe, when it drops on the land and re-mains until by fome movement of the earth a fmall fermentation is caufed, and vegetation takes place. One load of manure put in a ftate of fermentation into the land, is of double the value of the fame quantity, after it has been fuffered to lie until all fermentation is over, and has fhrunk to one half its bulk.

White-clover has been by fome fuppofed to caufe the rot in fheep. But in that cafe all the land in the world, capable of feeding fheep, muft caufe the rot. On the contrary, I am of opinion this diftemper is not occafioned by any fort of herb, but by a kind of egg or fpawn, frequently depofited in very fmall ftagnant fwamps of water. Thefe the fheep fwallow, and are not able to digeft : the liver affords them a neft in which they are hatched, and where the animalcula produced from them dwell, derive nourifhment from the blood, and increafe in bulk.

Having faid fo much on the three plants, rye-grafs, trefoil, and white-clover, under their
feparate

feparate heads; we fhall now confider them jointly. It is well known that all land will be more profitable by having a green crop one year, and a white crop another; and fo on alternately: therefore, as rye-grafs is a kind of white crop, like wheat or rye, and drawing a nourifhment different from that of trefoil or clover; it will, no doubt, be admitted that the three are proper to be fown together, and that they are thus likely to be more productive than any one of the forts fown feparate; for they affift each other, like true friends, throughout the feafon. Rye-grafs, by far the hardieft, peeps forth and foon rears its head in the fpring: as the mild weather advances, trefoil comes forward: and laftly the warm feafon ufhers in white-clover. At the time the white-clover approaches to maturity, the fun has a fcorching power extremely detrimental to it: but the mifchief is prevented by the fhade which the bent of the rye-grafs affords it.

Hay-feeds are very properly fo called; for they are indeed the feeds of hay, and confequently a collection of good, bad, and indifferent ftuff. They are fcarce ever to be met with free from a noxious mixture. How fhould

it

it be otherwife? By far the greateft part of
them are collected at inns in market-towns.
The mafter of the inn buys the coarfeft hay he
can procure, for fear his cuftomers' horfes
fhould over-gorge themfelves. One may often
hear fome of thefe landlords fay: "*That* hay
is too good for our market-horfes." So he
buys any rubbifh, provided it is not mouldy.
The oftler thrafhes the hay before he gives it
to the horfes, and fells the feeds as part of his
perquifites. Can the buyer then wonder at
having a plentiful crop of twitch and other
baneful weeds?

To procure the hay-feeds clean, the meadow
ought, in fummer, to be moft carefully weeded.
The mafter, or a man in whom he can confide,
fhould watch with a ftrict eye over the people
employed to weed; and the grafs fhould be
fuffered to ftand fufficiently long to ripen the
feed before mowing, fo as not to heat over
much in the ftack or mow. Some of the feed
will of courfe be deftroyed by the heat: but it
is the bufinefs of the grower to take care that
as little be damaged as poffible. When a ftack
of good hay is opened, the beft judge can
hardly diftinguifh the feeds that will grow from

thofe

thofe which have been fpoiled by too much heat: neither is it an eafy matter to afcertain the exact degree of heat neceffary to the perfection of hay.

Unlefs the farmer can depend upon his feed, how is he to know the quantity proper to be fown per acre? It is very common to hear him complain: " I fowed fuch a quantity of feed upon the land; but very little has grown!" Perhaps the feed was good for nothing—the land may not have been in a proper condition to receive it—or frofts may have deftroyed it. The miffing of a crop is moft probably owing to want of care in the procefs; for we know that feed will vegetate when put properly into the earth, provided the heart or germ of fuch feed be not injured.

It may not be fuperfluous to obferve, that hay-feeds, although light in themfelves, have confiderable gravity compared with the chaff or hulls which inclofe them. It is the cuftom to drefs thefe hay-feeds by a gentle wind; and the very *lighteft* are fold, though they confift of fcarce any thing but chaff. The fower fcatters, perhaps, eight bufhels of this ftuff per acre. But, alas! he fcratches his head with aſtoniſhment at having miſſed a good crop. However, as we take it for granted he ſowed little elſe than chaff, had he ſpread eighty buſhels per acre, the diſappointment would have been nearly the ſame.

When I firſt commenced farmer I did like my neighbours, and pinned my faith upon him who was moſt eſteemed as a good manager. When I ſaw ſome extraordinarily good graſs, I enquired how the owner managed it. I ſoon found that men of acknowledged abilities and experience differed in practice; and it ſtruck me that it might be poſſible to form a ſyſtem of my own, that I might avoid ſome things which they were wedded to by cuſtom, but which I ſaw ſtrong reaſons to diſapprove. In ſhort, being determined to think for myſelf, I tried a great number of experiments, and never ventured to recommend any new method to others until I had full proof of its efficacy from my own trials.

In time of ſeed-ſowing a dealer will offer hay-ſeeds for ſale, and will aſſert their goodneſs, though all his knowledge centres in having looked at them. If they are fair to the eye, that, in his opinion, conſtitutes perfection.

From

From the character I bear amongst the farmers of that part of the country I dwell in, I
am fuppofed to underftand feeds; and I have
been frequently applied to by the dealers or
venders for my approbation of their wares; as
they thought, that, if they could obtain my re-
commendation, they would find a ready market
for them. I muft own that I have frequently
diverted myfelf with the embarraffment of thefe
dealers, by taking out a feed promifcuoufly,
and enquiring the name of it. " Indeed, fir, I
cannot tell," is generally the anfwer. What
will it produce? " Oh, fir! that is quite uncertain." Nor does he know any one except
the rib-grafs, which is the plantain with a long
leaf, and which of all graffes I think the very
worft.

It would be a good method, and eafily ac-
complifhed, if a perfon would pick from a good
meadow fome of the very beft feed; then drefs
a fmall piece of land perfectly clean, as much
fo at leaft as you would for the choiceft flowers
in the garden; fow your feeds, and fave the
produce. They will quickly increafe fufficiently to fow a large field; and by a proper
degree of attention in eradicating weeds you
will

will foon have moft excellent grafs, and a conftant fupply of good hay-feeds, fuch as are not now to be met with. In all probability nothing in the farm would be found more advantageous than a meadow of fuch fort of grafs; for, if the farmer had more feed of this kind than neceffary for his own immediate ufe, he would find purchafers in plenty who would be glad to get it by paying a good price. Indeed, I recommend to the poffeffor of a farm of confiderable fize to grow all his own feeds of every fort or denomination; as it is a fafe way, and a great faving.

There are men who are bigoted to an opinion abfurd in the extreme: They fay, " Land ought to be fown with the fame as it produced before ploughing." But I fay, No; unlefs it produced better grafs, or at leaft as good as may be got elfewhere. Land of almoft every fort will improve by being ploughed up, provided fufficient care be taken to make the ftraw into manure, to lay it on in a proper manner, and to fow the different crops with judgment. All thefe things have been formerly but little attended to.

A piece of land laid down, and fown with grafs-feeds to lie for fward, will, from having

been

been ploughed and managed according to my rules, be enabled to produce better grafs than it did before, and of courfe will keep a greater number of fheep, cattle, horfes, &c. than if laid down with fhear-grafs, mofs, ling, gofs, &c. &c.

If a gentleman fuffers his tenant to plough up a piece of rich pafture-land with the intention of taking fix or eight crops from it; in all probability the tenant has fome poor worn-out ploughed land, and he makes the ftraw which grows on the frefh, into manure, and lays it on the poor land. The tenant fays, " The frefh land wants no manure; and poffibly he may be in the right. For, by beftowing on the old ploughed land the manure arifing from the new, he will derive from the former more abundant crops, and the latter will be fufficiently prolific without manure. By this method the farmer may improve his whole farm, and enrich the poor land confiderably, without impoverifhing that which he may have recently broken up.

Were the frefh rich land to be repaid all the manure which the poor ploughed land has at a former period borrowed; the rich land would not be impoverifhed by ploughing, but on the

contrary

ontrary much enriched. The tenant proves
his own enemy, if he exhaufts the rich land by
improper cropping, or by depriving it of all
the manure which has grown upon it, to enrich
other land. The landlord receives almoft as
much damage by this practice as if the ftraw
were fold from that land for fix or eight years;
and the tenant, after the land has been nearly
worn out, probably lays it down with a bad
kind of feed, or at leaft fomething which does
not vegetate! He then applies to the landlord
for leave to plough up another frefh piece; but
the landlord, if he knows his own intereft, an-
fwers " No! The clofe I fuffered you to plough
you have ruined; if I let you proceed, you
will fpoil the whole farm."

Suppofe we lay down what is commonly
called the worft mode of culture; and begin
by paring and burning—fow with rape-feed,
then wheat, then beans—the bean-crop in
drills. We fhall have fix loads of manure per
acre to lay in the drills, confequently fhall expect a very great crop of beans. Then wheat
again—then a crop of oats—then turnips.
Then we fhall have fix loads of manure from
thefe beans, wheat and oats, to lay on our tur-
nip-

nip-fallow. The turnips muft be eaten off by
fheep; and the next crop will be barley, and
grafs-feeds to lay down for a time. Now there
will have been the *afhes*, and *twelve* loads of
manure in fix years, which together are equal
to *fix* loads every other year; not taking into
the account the barley-crop, the ftraw of which
will in all probability amount to two loads
more of manure to return to this piece of land:
and were the two laft-mentioned loads worked
up with frefh earth into a good compoft, they
would produce four loads. If the land were
fown with rye-grafs, trefoil, and white-clover,
during the fummer, as large a quantity of feeds
would be fhed as ever were fown upon the land.
If the compoft were then fpread (four loads
per acre) and bufh-harrowed in, and the field
not depaftured during the winter; the feeds
fhed in the fummer would vegetate, with the
additional help and encouragement of the manure, and the land would be in no refpect injured by ploughing.

Having explained at length the method of
feeding land for grafs to lie for a confiderable
time, I recommend (as it is almoft impoffible
to procure hay-feeds of a proper fort, except
by

by the mean above pointed out) rye-grafs, trefoil, and white-clover; but particularly white-clover, where land is feeded to lie for a number of years. Not but that I think a fkilful botanift might collect from meadows the feeds of many graffes much preferable to rye-grafs, both for fattening cattle, and the long continuance of the crop, whether depaftured or mown. Thofe which abound more in leaf, which afford to the young fpringing grafs more fhade from the fcorching rays of the fummer fun, and the fucculent herbs, which collect the dews, and are fo charged with nutritive juices, would no doubt turn to more advantage.

SECTION XIV.

Method of Stocking the Seeds, or Mowing; and the Difference in Profit.

THE method of ftocking rye-grafs, whiteclover and trefoil, is defcribed under the foregoing article:

As to *red-clover*, it ought not to be eaten with any cattle whatever; for the young plants of clover are very tender. Above all, a horfe

ﬁhould

should not be suffered upon it; for by treading he will spoil more with his feet, than he devours with his mouth. This is easily proved to any farmer who may doubt of the fact, by turning loose any given number of horses into any quantity of land sown with clover; and, on the contrary, mowing an equal quantity, and stall or fold-feeding: he will find the advantage of fold-feeding to be four to one in his favour.

Cow-grass, being of the same nature, ought to be treated in the same manner as red-clover.

Lucerne ought not to be eaten while growing. It should be mown, and treated like a garden. It produces a wonderful profit, if used for stall-feeding; and, after being mown, it will immediately spring up again from the stumps. In making it into hay it should be treated like saintfoin: but care should be taken to mow it before it flowers: it is a sweet and very fattening food for cattle, who will eat it so greedily, that great caution must be used in giving them only a sufficient quantity at a time; otherwise they will swell and overload their stomachs with it till they burst, as they will with many other succulent plants. To avoid this, either give such

herbs

herbs fparingly, or mow them the day before you ufe them.

White-clover ought to be eaten by fheep.

Trefoil, which is itfelf a fpecies of clover, fhould alfo be eaten by fheep; for, if either this or white clover is mown for hay, there will be much lofs in the crops. The beft method, if intended for depafturing, is to fow it mixed with rye-grafs and white-clover: and if for mowing, with red clover. If for feeding fheep or cattle, I think it beft to mix red and white-clover together: but red-clover is the moft fattening.

From the pulpy nature of clover, the feet of cattle, or horfes, as we before obferved, will very much damage the plants. They bruife the young fprouts, and bruife them fo much as effectually to deftroy vegetation, at a time, perhaps, when the root protruded the laft fhoot: and the farmer thus finds himfelf deceived in his hopes of abundance. Let him therefore depafture it with fheep, foals, calves, or fome other ftock of light weight. A mixed ftock of fheep, young beafts and foals will pay beft. Pigs may likewife be turned in upon clover-fields: but it is more profitable to feed them in

the

the fold, for many reafons, which will be explained hereafter.

Yellow-clover is a fort I do not like; it being of a very poor nature, and its increafe not abundant, its leaf fmall, and its ftalk like wire.

SECTION XV.

Culture of Potatoes fully explained, by a new Syftem, on all Sorts of Soils.

I HAVE derived the greateft profits from planting the potatoes thick; nor do they thrive better by any method than by ploughing fward very thin, and fetting them under furrow about nine inches afunder. They do not thrive well when encumbered with too great a weight of earth: when fet under the fward, one furrow bearing upon another gives liberty to the fibres which are as fine as a hair and eafily obftructed, to run abundantly and freely, producing knots fpreading over the whole of the foil. After the potatoes have been fet, begin to harrow; and when they begin to appear through the feams, you muft harrow them again with the

utmoft

utmoft poffible care. Your own judgment muft be the guide as to the fort of harrow you make ufe of, and as to the time of doing it. It is next to impoffible to harrow them too well. I have feen an extraordinary crop on fward without harrowing it at all; but it certainly is the beft and fureft way not to omit it.

The above is a very cheap method of raifing potatoes, and perhaps the moft profitable of all others upon fward-land; for by the very fmothering crop, and the getting up of the potatoes at the latter end of the year, the foil is finely broken and reduced nearly to a pulverifed ftate, cheaper and fooner than by any other means; and confequently this is the readieft and beft mode of rendering it fit to receive corn.

If the land is covered with mofs, or with rough grafs, rufhes or haffocks, the method here prefcribed will be found to anfwer, though not fo well as paring and burning. The potatoes being ploughed up, and fcratched out of the ground by women and children, the roots become fo much loofened that it is eafy to harrow them out, and they may be quickly gathered up.

Where

Where the land is poor, if manure can be spared, it is proper to put it in with this crop, as the potatoes will thence doubtless grow much larger, and in greater abundance. And in the wheat crop the benefit will visibly appear again; therefore the farmer may be assured, the advantage of manure to this crop will be as great as to any one without exception.

The mode of setting potatoes on fallow land, is to clean the ground from all kinds of refuse stuff whatever, and then manure it with eighteen loads of manure per acre, if you have it. Spread it all over the land; plough, and make the furrows about sixteen inches wide; and in each furrow plant the potatoes from about six to nine inches asunder.

Twelve sacks will set an acre in my way: eight sacks is the usual quantity. I cut the potatoes, and leave two eyes in every *set*, if I can. In this way I have raised 180 sacks, or 2160 pecks per acre; in drills, never more than 100 sacks per acre. But then, when I followed the latter method, I used only twelve loads of manure per acre. One man and two horses, with the assistance of a man and six children, will plant six roods per day. The man must look after the children, lest they should

set

fet them over thin and improperly. There muſt be four women to rake the manure into the furrow; and the man ſhould watch them like-wiſe that they do it well. The potatoe muſt be laid upon the manure. This laſt is a moſt material and beneficial part of the proceſs; by attending to it, the produce will be much great-er than if you followed the oppoſite method.

If you have not ſufficient manure to cover the land, it is better to ſet the potatoes in drills, as they will make but poor progreſs upon moſt ſorts of ſoil without manure; except upon re-markably rich ground, or on ſward, and ſward-land the next year after it has been bro-ken up.

This is a crop I raiſe much cheaper, after ſet, than any fallow crop. I never hoe potatoes planted in my way. I let the land remain as left by the plough, until the weeds vegetate, which will be in ten days or a fortnight. I then harrow it over once or twice, ſo as to de-ſtroy the weeds. This harrowing will cauſe more to ſpring up: and theſe muſt, as ſoon as they appear, be in like manner deſtroyed. Con-tinue this proceſs till the potatoes are up, and, after they are up, until they are from three to four inches high. The harrowing may

injure

injure here and there a plant; but, as they are set so thick, it will do no material injury: on the contrary, it pulverises the soil, and leaves the potatoes every opportunity to grow and spread; so that in a short time their tops cover the land, and prevent any more weeds from growing that season. I have made land cleaner by this process than by any other I ever yet tried. Seldom a weed makes its appearance, and the few that do are easily destroyed; and when the potatoes are ploughed up, the women and children who gather them so separate the roots of every kind of weeds, that, by harrowing, they are very easily collected and carried off.

To get your potatoes out of the ground, you must first pull up all the tops and carry them off, and collect the potatoes that are pulled up along with them: then take a plough without a coulter, and plough the land deep enough to raise all the potatoes. You must have people sufficient to gather up every furrow, to keep the man and horses at work. The number of hands depends upon your crop. That done, you must with a pair of harrows with long teeth harrow the land well, to raise the potatoes

missed

miffed in gathering. When you fow your wheat, you muſt harrow again: there will be potatoes left worth gathering.

Potatoes for planting ought to be of a large ſize, as their eyes are ſtronger, and will produce a ſtronger plant, and bring a much larger produce; ſo much as to make the difference of thirty ſacks per acre betwixt large and ſmall potatoes for ſets.

It may be neceſſary to add, that all the ſpecies of potatoes may be managed according to the above methods, on all kinds of ſoil.

SECTION XVI.

Explanation why Wheat proſpers better after Potatoes than any other Crop.

AS the land is denſely covered and ſhaded by the potatoes all the hot dry ſeaſon, and when they are gathered by hand in autumn, is harrowed and much trodden, it becomes to a great degree pulveriſed; but yet preſerves a beneficial moiſture. At the ſame time the manure originally laid in for the potatoes intimately mingles with the ſoil, qualifies it to receive the

grain,

grain, and in the quickeſt and moſt perfect manner promotes vegetation. If the manure were put into the ground at the ſeaſon of ſow-ing wheat, it would lie in lumps, and act more partially; would add to the ſtraw, but little to the grain.

S E C T I O N XVII.

Different Kinds of Potatoes; Method of preſerv-ing them; their Uſe in feeding Cattle, Horſes, Pigs, Sheep, &c. Beſt Method of treating Stock ſo kept, by giving the Animals different Food at the ſame time.

THE ſorts of potatoe moſt productive to the planter, are, the ox-noble, the manly, the cham-pion, and the cluſter-potatoe.

The red-noſe kidney requires a good ſoil; but is apt to curl at top, ſo as to make it a precarious crop, unleſs the ſort is frequently changed.

There are many ſorts of potatoes beſides thoſe which I have enumerated; but amongſt the ſpecies into which this root is ſubdivided, none, in my opinion, is so productive as the ox-noble, nor any so good for the table as the kidney. I speak of the sorts now in use: but it is highly probable that by experiments in raising from seed, we may at some future time obtain potatoes superior to any at present known.

The best method of preserving potatoes is to make them into what is termed a *pie*. To make the pie, choose a dry piece of ground, dig it about eight inches deep, and lay the sods or mould so taken out bankwise on each side the intended pie; which will prevent the potatoes from running about. Let the pie be from six to nine feet wide at the base, and the sides fronting the east and west; one end only being exposed to the north. Raise it as high as you please, diminishing it to a sharp ridge, like the roof of a house or barn. If it be brought to a single row at the top, the pie will be the better for it. You must then cover the heap, first with straw, and then with mould regularly a foot thick: but if you add a greater thickness, you will better insure the safety of your pie from intense frosts, which, if suffered to penetrate, would spoil the whole. After incrusting your

pie

pie with a sufficient covering of mould, it will be most adviseable, as it is absolutely necessary to keep the contents dry, to thatch it in the same manner as a corn-stack. This will cause but little trouble, and effectually exclude rain and frost. Some, it is true, do not thatch them, and they may answer without: but it is safest not to omit that precaution; and I never think the trifling expence thrown away.

To wash potatoes, carrots, &c.—Take a vessel made in the form of a barrel-churn. The sides must be composed of pantile-laths, or something like them, nailed to the two ends, at such a distance from each other as to prevent the carrots or potatoes from falling out, and to suffer the water to pass freely through. A door must be left on one side, to put the carrots in and let them out at.

The vessel is hung over a square tub of water, so that about one half of it, and of the carrots, is immersed in water. You must turn it quickly round; and by these means you will soon wash great quantities of potatoes, carrots, turnips, &c. Fix the vessel over the tub in such a manner that when you have sufficiently washed your potatoes, you may lift it from the

part

part it turns in, to a higher one near to one side of the tub. Then open the door of the veffel, turn it round, and deliver the potatoes into a wheel-barrow.

Potatoes fhould not be given to horfes in large quantities: I do not approve of working horfes being fed with them.

Young horfes may thrive very well on potatoes: but it will be advifeable to give them either fome cut ftraw or other dry food at the time, as they are too juicy and cold of themfelves, although horfes are very fond of them. Many people boil or fteam potatoes for horfes, cattle, &c. but I do not approve of that practice, as they ftick in the teeth of the animal, and are difagreeable. I think it would be better if they were only juft warmed through. If cattle be fed on potatoes, chaff or chopped ftraw fhould be mixed with them, as they are liable to choak with eating potatoes alone. There have been numberlefs accidents of that kind: therefore precaution is neceffary.

Giving too large a quantity at one time may prove of great detriment: this caution muft be attended to, not only in refpect to potatoes, but many forts of green food, fuch as the different

ferent kinds of clover, faintfoin, lucerne, &c.
&c. It is, indeed, not furprifing that animals
fhould over-gorge themfelves, when the food
is green and lufcious to their tafte: but I had
once a fine young horfe, who, by flipping his
halter in the ftable, got to the corn-bin, and
fo immoderately ftuffed himfelf with oats, that
he was unable to digeft them, and died within
lefs than twenty-four hours. Dry food given
at intervals, whilft they feed occafionally upon
green, will be found the beft method of treating thefe kinds of animals: always taking care
to be profufe in neither fort.

Sheep are very fond of potatoes; yet I never
knew them over-feed upon them: but doubtlefs
they may, as they frequently do upon turnips.

Cows fed with potatoes produce much better milk and butter, than when they eat cab-
bage or turnips.

SECTION XVIII.

*Method of harvefting Grain of all Kinds, with
Proofs from actual Experiments.*

THE reaping corn from ten to fourteen
days earlier than my neighbours, is an advantage I have lately attended to. As corn begins

to

to decay firſt at the root, all the nouriſhment it can afterwards receive while it ſtands uncut muſt be derived from the ſtraw. The dews may feed the grain at one time; but, when nearly ripe, and the root gone, the ſun and wind have ſo much power as to ripen it too quickly, or to ſcorch it up before its natural period of maturity. How often do the *old* farmers complain, that the ſeaſon of harveſt is ſo dry that the corn will all be ſmall! There would be little cauſe for this complaint, if they cut the corn earlier, and put the ſheaves into ſtooks in the field, which would ſecure it from the intenſe heat of the ſun, and from thoſe violent winds that ſo frequently occaſion great loſſes by ſhaking the grain out of the ear before reaped.

Once, by chance, riding on the road about harveſt-time, I ſaw a field of wheat that had taken the mildew. This is known by the ſtraw being of a remarkably deep green, and, inſtead of dying, appearing to revive and acquire a greater verdure; which plainly indicates that the nutritive ſap ſtagnates, and that the grain receives from it no further nouriſhment. Nor does it, after ſuch appearance comes on, ever

receive

receive any, or grow larger. The straw becomes spotted and black. The sooner then it
is cut, the better I took twelve ears of the
wheat, which, as likewise the straw, were green
as grafs, and mildewed. A great deal of rain
had fallen the fore part of the day; but the
wheat-ears were pretty dry. I tied them in a
bunch, intending to hang them up in some dry
place to ripen; but on my return home forgot,
and thought no more about them. My great
coat, being used only when there was reason to
expect rain, was hung up in a hall; and several
weeks afterwards, on putting my hand into one
of the pockets, I found the ears of wheat, which
immediately brought the circumstance to my
recollection. The straw still remained green.
I rubbed out the grain; and, to my astonishment, never saw better. It was fine in colour,
and well filled; but what remained in the field
I took these ears from, was very small, and of
little value.

From this it would appear, that were wheat
cut on the appearance of the mildew, and set
in the field in small stacks of about a cart-load
each, so as neither to heat nor mould, it might
render it much better than is done by the method

thod now practifed. Indeed the mildew in
wheat is like the mildew on all other things.
It is caufed by damp in the foil. Very warm
dry fituations feldom have any mildewed wheat:
as in a warm dry room your paper or linen is
not mildewed; confequently, after your wheat
is perceived to be getting into that ftate, the
fooner it can be preferved from it the better.

I had taken at the fame time twelve ears of
wheat from an adjoining field riper, which I
put in the other pocket of my great coat. Thefe
laft, though at the time of gathering they appeared fo much fuperior to thofe which had
taken the mildew, did not turn out nearly fo
good as the others. The reafon appeared plain
to me: the ripe wheat had ftood too long, and
the wind and fun had fhrivelled it up, and caufed
it to be fmall.

From the above circumftances I have ever
fince been partial to cutting wheat when the
ftraw appears of a reddifh caft, or fome of it
green, and the joints are full of fap: and it always has fulfilled my expectations; for the
ftraw, if intended for chaff, will be better, the
flour much fairer and heavier; and if intended
for fine flour, it will grind into broad bran
much

much better than that harvested according to the old method. I do not however think that wheat which has not taken the mildew ought to be cut fo green.

Rye fown along with wheat is a great preventative of the mildew; for rye is of a much drier nature, and moft certainly prevents fo much damp rifing to the ftraw of the wheat, It is evident the damp rifes upwards; for if you build a houfe upon a wet or damp foundation, all the fun and air in the univerfe will not fufficiently make it comfortably dry and warm. You will find fwamps on a field more fubject to mildew than the more elevated parts. I have fown rye mixed with wheat upon one piece of a field, and on the next wheat only; and the wheat amongft the rye was fcarcely damaged, and the other in a very bad condition from the mildew. As the damp from the earth is the principal caufe of this malady in corn, the beft remedy is to drain the land, and to lay on it manure of the drieft nature, fuch as bones, afhes, &c.

There are other proofs of the damp from the earth caufing the mildew; fuch as, that other white corn is not fo much, or feldom at all, attacked by it. Wheat being fown in autumn, and lying fo long on rhe land, the foil has not fo good an opportunity to get dried afrer the winter, by being expofed to the fun and air. It may likewife be obferved, that, in years when the feafon has caufed the leaf to be more abundant, and to fmother the land the moft, the mildew is moft prevalent. Late crops are more given to this malady; and the caufe is the foil's getting damper. I do not recollect to have feen fpring wheat take the mildew; owing, I fuppofe, to its lying a lefs time on the ground.

Oats for meal, if early reaped, are much finer in colour; the ftraw is better; and there is lefs lofs in the field.

Barley, by being cut foon enough, becomes much better for malting; even though cut fo early that fome part of it may not be ripe. Were you to let it ftand until it were all ripe, it would ftill differ in refpect to the dying or ripening of part; confequently, when wetted to undergo the neceffary procefs for malting, as it died at different times, fo will it have different times of refurrection or fprouting. Killing it all at one time by art, may enable the

maltfter

maltſter by art again to revive it, perhaps on the ſame day—a deſireable acquiſition in making malt to perfection; for if one grain begins to vegetate before another, part will be ready for the kiln before the reſt; and when the maltſter hopes to have the whole in a proper ſtate for drying, thoſe grains which had firſt vegetated would be acre-ſpired, and the ſaccharine quality be reduced at leaſt one fifth— a loſs which would be heavily felt by the brewer.

In peas—a great advantage ariſes from cutting early. The ſtraw, being full of leaf, makes excellent fodder; and, if there be wet weather, it does not occaſion the pods to open ſo ſoon. I do not approve of ſheafing peas, or tying them up; a mode chiefly made uſe of in Scotland. By drilling with manure, the ſtraw will be very long, and of courſe require a different method of reaping. My peas were from ten to twelve feet long, laſt year, podded from top to bottom, and yielded forty buſhels per acre: a very great produce, as they were of the Haſtings kind, which are very ſmall. They were reaped with ſickles, ripping them up for a few feet, then pulling them from the ſtanding ones,

laying

laying the green end down, and the bottom upwards, and lapping the pods as much inwards as poffible. By this method, the green part dried gradually: and pigeons, which frequently deftroy much of this crop if they can get to the pods, were prevented from doing much damage.

It is beft to mow barley, and let it lie in the fwath for fome days before you fheat it; as every poffible precaution fhould be ufed to prevent mow-heating.

Oats are beft mown, and bound in fheaves after the fcythe, and left upon the ground, not fet up in ftooks, as commonly practifed. But the people who bind them muft give them a turn over; as the fide they tie them on would readily receive the wet, but on the other fide it cannot get in. By laying that fide upwards, no rain will injure them for a long time; and they will *harveft* much quicker than in the ftook; as the wind will have a free paffage through the bottom, which requires the moft air: whereas, if fet in the ftook, it would be a long while before they were fit to carry; and if left in the fwath, fhould the weather prove wet, great part would be loft by turning over.

Beans

Beans are generally mown; but I approve of pulling them up: as the roots are very injurious to a wheat-crop, so much so as to prevent wheat being sown; on account of snails crawling into the land and destroying the wheat. The expence is little different. They should be tied up in sheaves with wheat-straw. If they stand till the leaf decay, tie them loosely in small bunches, and set them up in stooks (four sheafs to the stook) in the field, where they will soon be fit for carrying home; for the leaf being gone, the wet will not remain upon them, and the bean will retain its proper colour, which otherwise would become black. Let them be stacked upon a belfry or tuffel, and they will receive for a long time no injury, as the air freely penetrates.

SECTION XIX.

Method of preserving Crops, after reaped, to the greatest Advantage, when Barns are not large enough for such Crops.

TO preserve corn expeditiously and safely, must no doubt be desireable. On a fine day, when corn is ready to be carried, it is an excellent

cellent method to ftack it in the field where it grew; for by fo doing you will probably fecure as much in *one* day, as you would have been able to carry home in *four*; or, if the diftance be confiderable, perhaps in a week. And if rain fhould come the next day, or foon after, and continue, this manner of proceeding may be of very great convenience and advantage; it may make in the corn the difference of *good*, and of *good for nothing*; but to a certainty that of *good* and *indifferent*.

It may not perhaps be unneceffary to fay how a ftack fhould be conftructed, fo as to be liable to the leaft inconvenience. Begin to make the middle of the ftack firft, fo that, when it is taken in, the middle muft be fulleft: the outfide fheaves will then act as thatch; and even if the ftack were not thatched, no common rain of fhort duration could injure one fo made. But fuppofing it tolerably, or what the thatcher would call *well* thatched, it is poffible rain may penetrate; but if it did, the corn would receive little injury, as the moifture, from the conftruction here laid down, would entirely ooze out: nor can rats, mice, or many other vermin which frequently caufe havock amongft corn do fo much damage in a ftack fo made.

Another

Another advantage attending the making of a ſtack in an open field is, that the grain by the free circulation of air becomes ſoon dry, and preſerves the original ſweetneſs; whereas in confined places, ſuch as *ſtack-garths*, where great numbers of ſtacks ſtand cloſe together, or in *barns*, the air frequently ſtagnates, and the corn becomes muſty, or acquires a putrid ſmell.

The above method will be found to anſwer for corn in general.

SECTION XX.

The Author's Opinion on Tranſplanting Wheat: Reaſons why it muſt prove beneficial.

TRANSPLANTING of wheat, ſo as to ſet a whole field, is not likely to become a general practice: but circumſtances frequently occur where it may be attended with ſome benefit. For example, when ſome misfortune happens to a part of the field, a diligent obſerver will generally diſcover ſome ſpots to have miſſed, and to be thinner than the others. Whatever may have been the cauſe of the ground's ground's not being regularly covered, whether the wheat's having been deftroyed by water in the winter, or from any other accident; the farmer may always find fome part of the fame field from whence he may draw plants without doing any harm; and if he be a neat hufband-man, he may fill up the vacancies by tranfplant-ing from thofe fpots where the plants are fo thick as to injure each other.

SECTION XXI.

Advantage of Dibbling Wheat.

THE great advantage of dibbling wheat is in the treading of the light land by people pafs-ing and repaffing; for the regularity of fowing is not fo great, children often dropping in twenty grains inftead of four. I much approve of the practice on all flag land or fwards plough-ed up for clover, hay, &c.; for the men or women ftepping backward upon every furrow to make the holes, and the children to depofit the wheat, tread the land down fo that it has an immediate connection with the ramel. The grain is depofited where it ought to be, in the

beft

beſt of the ſurface ſoil, about three inches aſunder every way, and about one inch and half deep in each furrow; ſo that it juſt reaches the beſt part of the ſurface ſoil to derive its ſupport from. Should your ploughman *turn-over* twelve inches, four rows of wheat ought to be ſet on each furrow: and to do this, the iron or dibble might have two prongs. It is not indeed uſual to plough the furrow twelve inches broad: but, for dibbling, I do not think the furrow can be too broad, provided the plough clears her way and lays it flat. The ſeed in the broad-caſt falls where it ought not to do, betwixt the furrow, where the ſoil being light continually keeps dropping from the root, ſo that it is left without proper nouriſhment, by which means the growth of the plant is retard-ed, and the produce diminiſhed. On the con-trary, when dibbled, the root ſtands upon the firm earth, and the worms or grubs, &c. are in ſome meaſure deprived of the immediate op-portunity of feeding on it.

Eight pecks of ſeed might, if properly de-poſited, be ſufficient for dibbling one acre. Ten pecks is what I ſhould uſe. I am no friend to the ſaving of ſeed; as on every experiment

I have tried, the lofs of produce in both ftraw and corn greatly furpaffed the value of the feed faved. Some ufe in dibbling only fix pecks per acre. But this certainly is too fmall a quantity; for many of the grains fall by the fides of the holes, and grow not up to perfection. However, among dibbled wheat you will find the feweft fmall and light ears.

The expence of dibbling is with fome an objection. Individually it cofts money; but publicly it cofts nothing, becaufe it is done chiefly by women and children, who muft be maintained from the produce of the earth; and is it not better that the women and children fhould work for their meat and clothing, than to have it found them for nothing? And in the proper feafon for dibbling wheat there is no other fort of work for them. The expence is from 9s. to 10s. 6d. per acre.

Some may fay, " Clay foils it will injure." But I fay, no. For, during the winter the frofts lighten the foil; and on fwards or clover-ley there is a mellownefs which prevents them from being of too binding a nature. It might be an improvement in the prefent practice, with the fkim-plough thinly to pare the fod or ftubble, and

and lay them in the bottom of the furrow; as that would prevent all kinds of grafs or weeds from making their appearance: and then the broader the furrow the better.

Dibbling of fpring-corn, where land is liable to fet or bake, may be attended with fome of thefe inconveniences. Therefore, judgment is required in the fpring to diftinguifh the fort of land proper for dibbling.

Oats, peas, and beans ought all to be dibbled; as harrowing them brings them to the top as it does ftones: and it is impoffible to cover them properly, but by dibbling or drilling.

The neceffary operations for dibbling are as follow: Plough the land in broad furrows as deep as the foil will admit, afterwards roll it. Then a man or woman takes a couple of irons, and going backwards makes two holes at one time, one with each hand. The dibbling-irons are fixed to handles of a proper length: and the point muft be fo contrived as to make the holes one inch and a half wide, and one inch and a half deep: then put in the feed about four grains in each hole: then bufh-harrow two or three times lengthwife, and then acrofs the lands. If a flock of fheep were driven acrofs

the

the field, it would be of great ufe, as the feet
of the fheep would tread the earth into the holes
where the feed is depofited, and prevent the
water from lodging in them. After the fheep
are removed from the field; bufh-harrow again.

SECTION XXII.

Ufe and Advantage of Drilling Wheat.

DRILLING of wheat is a great faving of
grain. No one can doubt of this affertion
being a fact; as by it the feed may be put into the ground in a regular manner, either as
to depth or diftance. It may likewife be made
ufe of for all other kinds of grain: and I think
the faving of feed would be at leaft one third.
As to fcarifying afterwards, that feems of little
ufe except in land that is apt to *bake* and
crack—See Section VII.

There cannot be a doubt but all corn ought
to be depofited a certain depth in the ground,
and at certain diftances: therefore, to do that,
the land muft be firft pulverized and made
ready to receive its crop; and then the corn

put

put in it. It little matters by what mode this is done; the more fimple the better. The drill-roller does its work with as much defpatch as any thing I have feen, and fully as well. It may be neceffary to defcribe it (fimple as it is) to thofe who have not feen it. It is a roller, of any given length, made of wood, with nicks cut in it about fix inches afunder, as deep as your timber will properly admit. The edges muft be fhod with iron rather fharp, that when it turns round it may make fmall furrows or drills proper for your grain to fall in. You muft fow it broad-caft, and bufh-harrow the land after-wards. As to depth, you muft add more weight to your rollers, if you fee it not penetrate far enough. It is a good way to fix at the back-part of the roller fomething to clean out the nicks, or they will clog up and not make drills fufficiently deep to receive the grain. I have feen fome very regular good crops, that had been fown in this way.

SEC-

SECTION XXIII.

What Horses most proper for Husbandry; Instructions for Breeding them; of their Shape, Action, &c.

THE horse used in husbandry ought to be larger, but in other respects like the road-horse: and, instead of walking two or three miles an hour, he ought to walk four or five. In that case, he would be able both to plough more land in a given time, and would work in the cart or waggon with more dispatch, when wanted. In harvest time a nimble and strong horse is valuable. In drawing manure into the field, or corn to market, the farmer will also find his account in strength and activity: for, as the draught in all these cases is light one way, such horses would do their business with speed. The small farmer need not with this kind of horse keep an idle one; he might carry his master to market, and plough the remainder of the week. This is the sort of horse proper for a gentleman's heavy coach: therefore, if the farmer should determine to breed, and take a little pains to rear horses of bone and action, it

would

would not only prove advantageous to himſelf, but uſeful to the public.

Theſe horſes ſhould be bred to be from fifteen to ſixteen hands high, ſhould walk light five miles an hour, trot twelve; and if one now and then turned out rather low, he would notwithſtanding fetch a good deal of money for carrying ſome heavy gentleman.

Horſes of this deſcription are hardy, and require leſs food to ſupport them than the long-waiſted waſhy things of faſhion, which ſome half connoiſſeurs in horſe-fleſh are ſo fond of.

The general opinion is, that, if a horſe is put to draw, it will make him ſtumble. If he is over-weighted and worn down, this poſſibly may be true: but keep a horſe above his work, and he will be no worſe for the ſaddle. I have a proof of this in a mare I now ride. She is of the breed I recommend. I bought her, when ſhe was four years old, out of a man's team, which he worked for hire. He had drawn her two years very hard, yet ſhe has carried me (though I ride nineteen ſtone) nine years, and has never once been down with me, although I have ridden her over as dangerous roads as any in the kingdom—in Derbyſhire, Cheſhire,

Lan-

Lancashire, Westmoreland, &c. I do not now think her, as to safety, in any respect worse than when I bought her: on the contrary, I really think her better. I gave eighteen pounds for her, which was thought too high a price by some who pretended to be judges: but I have many time since been bid fifty pounds for her, and once absolutely sold her for sixty; but the gentleman to whom I sold her, at my own earnest request, let me have her again for the same money. She will carry my weight ten miles an hour with ease. I have ridden her from Lincoln to Doncaster, which is forty-two miles, within five hours. This mare was bred from one of the cart kind, and got by a blood-horse. The service she has done makes me so strenuously advise breeding this sort of horses, which will in all probability turn out so useful to the breeder and to the public.

SECTION XXIV.

Description of a Road-Horse; particular Action necessary for the Ease and Safety of the Rider.

THE road-horse should have a small head, a quick eye, with a rising forehand or neck; his shoulder to be cast into his back, not very fine

in

in the chine. His back muſt be ſtraight, not over
ſhort. Let him be high in his ribs, and ſtraight
in his hind quarters, his hucks lying cloſe
or round with his rib, and his tail ſtanding
ſtraight with his quarter; thick in his thigh,
and broad in his breaſt; ſhort in his legs,
with his fetlock very ſhort; a good round
hoof, not over ſteep. He ſhould rather ſtand
a little out with his fore toes, and his hind feet
the ſame; for by that poſition he is both ſtronger and ſafer. He cannot move with one leg
too near the other, provided he does not cut.
For, when a horſe moves, he muſt have two
legs off the ground: therefore by keeping his
legs near each other he is ſtronger. By one
leg on the ground being perpendicular, and
his toes ſtanding a little out, he is much ſafer:
if he makes a trip, he does not ſo ſoon loſe his
balance, or get over his knee. The ſhorter he
ſteps the better, if he is but quick (for light
moving is equal to ſtrength); and by keeping
his legs under him, he does not tire like a
horſe who overſteps and fatigues himſelf. Nor
does he beat the ground ſo hard; ſo that his
feet and legs laſt much longer.

SEC-

SECTION XXV.

Beſt Method of Shoeing the Road-Horſe, to em-
power him to travel with Eaſe and Comfort
to himſelf.

THE foot of a horſe ſhould be kept in
the ſame form it had when he was foaled; the
toe ſhort, and the heel up. The ſhoe ſhould
not be longer than the hoof of the toe, and the
leaſt that is poſſible in the heels. For, if you
ſhoe him much longer at the heel than the corner, that part of the ſhoe acts like a lever behind his heel, as if you meant to lame him by
prizing it with a crow, or bar of iron. Indeed
the ſhoe of a horſe ought to cover little or no
more ground than his foot would if not ſhod;
for if it does, it will only ſerve to break his
hoof, draw out the nails and looſen the ſhoe;
as, if he treads the leaſt uneven, which is frequently the caſe, the ſuperfluous iron acts in
the way juſt mentioned.

If the horſe's hoof is naturally hollow, the
ſhoe ſhould be thickeſt near the edge or nail-
holes.

If he have a flat, or what is termed an *oyſter*
foot, the ſhoe on the contrary ought to be diſh-

ed,

ed, as in that fort of foot the quick lies near, and of courfe he muft be tender. Bar fhoes are proper for fuch feet.

SECTION XXVI.

Defcription of the Dray-Horfe, and the Stage-Waggon-Horfe to travel.

DRAYS require the floweft movement in a horfe. The burthens are generally exceffively heavy; in London ftreets particularly, where no fwiftnefs, but great power is required to move the immenfe weights drays are often loaded with. Horfes for this purpofe, therefore, fhould be very broad-breafted, and thick in the fhoulders, which fhould not lie backward. Nor fhould the fore-hand be up as recommended in the road-horfe; for, by holding up their heads, they would be choaked by the collar, as they would, if fo formed, draw too much by the throat, and their wind being thus ftopped, would be in danger of falling down. The neck of a dray-horfe is not the better for being long. If his head be fmall, he is likely to be of better thrift; but then on the other hand, a fmall head is fometimes a fign of a

lively

lively fpirit, which makes a horfe not fteady in drawing; and it is a great fault in a dray-horfe to be quick or hafty in temper. Like all horfes, he fhould be chofen with fhort legs, and good ftrong hoofs. He ought to be thick in his thighs, and large in bone: but I can fee no neceffity for that great quantity of hair fo frequently met with upon the legs of thefe animals. I am of opinion, that, in refpect to ufe, he would be better without that fuperfluous ornament: but perhaps, the dealer would not give fo good a price for him without the hair, as with: therefore, as breeders, like other men, muft look to their profit, they will no doubt continue to rear fuch horfes as will fetch moft at market, and think more of fhow than real ufe; for a redundancy of hair is not a fure indication of ftrength.

Moft of the obfervations laid down refpecting the dray-horfe are equally applicable to the ftage-waggon horfe. His fhape and make, however, muft not be exactly the fame; for, as the waggon-horfe is required to travel, he muft partake of the nature both of the true dray-horfe, which originally was a native of Flanders, and of the true Englifh coach-horfe, a breed unknown anywhere but in this ifland.

A

A quicker movement is required for a ftage-waggon than for a dray, and fomething more of fpirit in the horfe. A true dray-horfe could not laft long in a waggon; as he is rather too heavy.

SECTION XXVII.

Opinion on Draught Oxen; the Sort for fuch Ufe.

THE Devon ox is a pattern, as to make and fhape, for all draught-oxen The Devon-fhire ox is better formed to move than any fort I have feen, excepting the Scotch ox, called the Fifefhire ox, which is made better in refpect to walking than any other; for he has the beft feet I ever met with. The Welfh ox is in ma-ny refpects fimilar to the Scotch.

The ox moftly ufed by our farmers is of the Tees-water or Durham, and the Holdernefs fpecies.

The Devonfhire oxen are as good, if not better feeders than any fort I have yet feen: they attain very heavy weights, and cut up as fine as any, without exception.

The Fifefhire fattens not fo quickly as the Devonfhire ox; but, when fat, is equally de-licious.   The

The Tees-water ox is proper for heavy draughts, is much larger in fize, and will pay better for his keep. He may draw from the age of *two* to that of *eight*; if fattened when two years old, he may weigh about forty ftone; if made fat at the age of eight, he will weigh ninety ftone or more. Suppofing beef at feven fhillings per ftone, the difference between flaughtering him at the age of two, and at that of eight years will be as 14*l.* to 31*l.* 10*s.* that is, 17*l.* 10*s.* for the keep of the ox for fix years, which is 2*l.* 18*s.* and a fraction per year.

Now it is well known the horfe frequently decreafes as much in value. But is not that the farmer's fault? For horfes may be made to pay for their meat as well as oxen. A mare, for example, may breed a foal, and do a great deal of work; in the winter at this rate fhe may be reckoned at about 6*l.* per year. In fummer an ox is kept at a cheap rate, and may fupply her place. A young horfe, bought in with judgment, and worked eafily, will pay two guineas per year, on the loweft eftimate. A horfe will not thrive upon fuch food as will keep an ox; but if you work an ox with a horfe fide by fide, the ox muft be fed with corn in the winter. After all, the advantage is clearly on

the

the fide of the ox; unlefs you fell the horfe when he comes juft into his prime. For, if you wear the horfe out, his flefh is fit only for the dogs, and the carcafe with the fkin will not fetch more than a dozen or fifteen fhillings, whilft an ox will fetch from 20*l*. to 30*l*. or perhaps much more. I think that farmer the beft manager who keeps both horfes and oxen for draught; for he will thus be enabled to fend the moft commodities to market from any given quantity of acres of land.

There is a fort of oxen which I have not yet defcribed, which are the long-horned or Craven kind: thefe oxen are bad workers, but in general pay beft when killed very young—at the age of three years, for example. Therefore they feldom draw or plough much. The Irifh oxen, whith refpect to working, are very fimilar to the Craven kind.

It has been afferted that an ox will plough as much land in any given time as a horfe: but that is impoffible, if the horfe be of the right fort for the plough. The horfe would certainly walk over three miles while the ox walks over two, therefore would plough three acres of land whilft the ox ploughs two acres. I believe,
that

that at prefent the ox does as much work in any given time as the horfe; but that is either the fault of the mafter or the man; for the maf-ter muft either have provided a horfe of very flow movement, or the man muft be very idle. I will undertake to find a man and pair of hor-fes to plough three acres while another man and a pair of oxen ploughs two acres, for twelve months together. But then we muft confider the difference of expence in their feeding, and of the value of the carcafe of the worn-out horfe and the worn-out ox, as has been re-marked above. Both are very ufeful, and ought always to form part of the ftock of a farm of confiderable extent.

A man in a very fmall farm, confifting of from eight to twenty acres fhould work his milch-cows, or fuch as he may be rearing for that purpofe. By tilling his fmall quantity of land to advantage, he might keep eight or ten cows, and get fifteen acres of corn every year; which, at 10l. per acre, would make 150l. be-fides the profit of the cows, which might be managed in fuch a way as to injure them ve-ry little, as there are fo many to do fo little work.

The

The ox, I will allow, is not the moſt pleaſ-
ant animal to do huſbandry buſineſs with: the
farmer's ſervant will diſcover as much difference between the horſe and ox in this reſpect,
as he would between the horſe and aſs, were
he obliged occaſionally to uſe both for a journey: but the pleaſure of the ſervant in that
caſe has been more conſidered than the profit
of the farmer. The horſe paſſes quickly over
the ground; and, in a bad ſeed-time, when
land is liable to *ſet*, become hard, or over-wet,
getting the ſeed in quickly in the proper ſeaſon is of infinite conſequence to a crop; and,
oxen being ſlow, the farmer muſt either employ
an extra number of them, or beſtow more time
in ſowing his crop, or in doing any other kind
of buſineſs.

SECTION XXVIII.

*Milch-Cows proper for the Dairy, and for
Fattening.*

THE cow which gives the moſt milk is
not the cow which fattens the faſteſt. It is
impoſſible ſhe can vie in fleſh with the cow
which gives only a ſmall quantity, and whoſe
food is principally applied to the fattening of

her.

her. The draining of nutritive juices by milking muſt, with very few exceptions, keep the
milch-cow down: and the ſame obſervation
will hold good reſpecting the quick-feeding
or faſt-fattening cow, which will always be
found to be ſcanty of milk.

The features of good milch-cows, and of
thoſe for fattening, are nearly the ſame. A
cow for milking ought to have a ſmall head,
a thin hide, fine chaps, a ſmall tail, the thighs
thin, and of ſmall bone. Her paps ſhould
hang ſquare; the udder ſhould be round, and
not fleſhy; her milk-vein very ſtrong. The
vein called the milk-vein runs upwards from
the udder towards the huck. There are cows
of a different deſcription, which yet are good
milkers: but the above ſort will be found of
moſt general uſe. Some very ill-ſhaped cows
give a large quantity of milk; but, for the moſt
part, they have a ſmall tail and thin chaps.

The cow with a diſpoſition to fatten faſt differs from the milch-cow by the milk-vein
being much ſmaller, and the udder appearing
leſs, and of courſe containing leſs milk: her
hide, if thick and mellow, is a ſign of her thriving; and what is termed a thin or paper hide
covers generally a poor animal and a bad
thriver.   SEC·

SECTION XXIX.

Method of Fattening Calves to the best Advantage:

TO make calves fat in the speediest manner, take the milk from the cow and boil it, and let it stand to be cool enough for the calf to drink. By this method the flesh will become white without bleeding; the veal will be juicy, have a good flavour, and be much better for eating, than the calf whose juices had been so much exhausted and dried by frequent bleedings, that the flesh has no more nourishment in it than the pith of a willow-stick. It is very proper to give the calf in the middle of the day a ball or two mixed up with common gin, which not only will promote sleep, but will prevent the milk from turning sour on his stomach, and like-wise keep his body regularly open. A small glass of gin is sufficient to wet flour enough for two balls; and no other ingredients are required. These balls are not to be used before the calf is a month old. The calf cannot be kept in too close a place: he should be well bedded with clean straw; and the place where he stands should be made slanting, so that all

wet

wet immediately run off; for, if he lies wet, he lies cold; and great care ought to be taken that he lie dry and warm. I have fed a calf that at the age of thirteen weeks has produced, when flaughtered, 8*l.* 19*s.* 6*d.* This calf weighed feventy pounds per quarter.—See Annals of Agriculture, No. 155, p. 557.

SECTION XXX.

Ufe of Sheep in Improving Land: the great Profit arifing therefrom.

SHEEP are the moft profitable of animals; as they not only increafe in flefh much quicker than moft others, but pay a yearly tribute to the owner by their fleeces. They fupply us with a ftaple commodity, which employs an infinite number of people at home, and produces a moft beneficial trade abroad.

Where fheep eat the herbage, they manure land very regularly, and caufe the grafs to come finer after than when eaten by any other animal I know, except deer.

Sheep by nature are cleaners of land. To maintain themfelves, they will eat every kind

of

of weed, except nettles and thistles, and confequently eat to greater profit than any other animal. The lofs in fheep is attended with lefs lofs of property than generally attends the lofs of other animals which are accounted as ftock by the farmer: the fkin at every age is of fome value; and fo is the flefh in many inftances, when you have a careful and attentive fhepherd. They are very prolific, and begin breeding early. I have bought a drape-ewe in September, and by the September following with two lambs fhe paid clear profit 3*l.* 16*s.* when fold to the butcher. I bought her in at 1*l.* 4*s.* She fold for 2*l.* 5*s.*; the fleece for 5*s.*; the two lambs for 1*l.* 5*s.* each; which together makes five pounds. Deducting then the original coft of 1*l.* 4*s.* I have a clear balance of 3*l.* 16*s.* Two fuch ewes would bring 7*l.* 12*s.* profit: one acre of good land would keep them, and fufficient bite be left for a horfe or beaft to defray all expences.

By expending 2*l.* 8*s.* in the purchafe of two fheep, a clear profit may be gained of 7*l.* 12*s.* I know of no other animal that will do as much upon one acre of land with fo little rifque of capital;

capital; as, in cafe of accident, you in all
probability have the chance of feveral lives,
and the original coft is but trifling.

SECTION XXXI.

Defcription of the beft Sort of Sheep, with In-
ftructions for Breeding them; the Sort of
Wool required, and how to promote the
Growth of it.

THE Diſhley ſheep are without difpute the
beft. The breed is now fo univerfally fpread
over this ifland, that it might be thought fuperfluous to defcribe them; but as this work may
poffibly be read in other countries befides England, I think it neceffary to give a fketch of
this very ufeful animal. A true Diſhley ſheep
from the top of the back, that is, from head to
tail, refembles the back of a tortoife; the head
is fmall; the neck or crag particularly fo,
and fo ſhort that, when the fheep is hung up
by the heels, you cannot fee any neck; the
fat and fleſh fo completely covering it that the
fore-quarter appears as if joined to the head.
The breaft is remarkably wide or broad; the
car-

carcafe not very long; but the rib ftands up well (that is, high and round), fo that by laying your hand upon him you will perceive an extraordinary breadth. He is much inclined to accumulate flefh upon the back : the fat of many of them upon the ribs and fides hangs in fuch a manner as to caufe what is called the fore-flank and the neck-vein to be larger than you can grafp with your hand; fomething like a bullock's flank, but very frequently fuller, except it be a very fat bullock. I have feen mutton of this kind cut fix inches deep on the rib. In his twift he will be fo cloven between the legs as almoft to touch his *camerils*. In fhort, the offal (fuch as the fhanks, neck, and head) of this fort of fheep, which weighs from thirty to forty pounds per quarter, will weigh but few pounds ! And what renders it ftill more an object of profit is, that it not only eats lefs than any other kind, but from its propenfity to thrive becomes fat much fooner.

Were thefe fheep kept poor upon thin lands, on commons of a dry gravel or limeftone foil, until they were four or five years old (as fome of the Downs and Scotch fheep are), and then made fat, I have no doubt but the mutton
would

would be full of gravy, and the beſt in the
world; as they are remarkably juicy and fine-
grained. Many gentlemen have obſerved to
me that ſheep of this kind are liable to get
over-fat; and that the flavour of the mutton is
not ſo delicate as that of ſome other ſorts. My
anſwer is, that ſheep of this kind are at preſent
in the hands of the beſt feeders, as well as
breeders; and as the price of the ram is very
high, great care is in general taken of the off-
ſpring—ſuch care that they are frequently kept
fat the whole time they live, ſometimes too
much ſo; which cauſes their fleſh to become
ſtrong: and this I believe to be the caſe in all
animals when they attain a certain age. I had a
ſtriking proof of this, in regard to the flavour
of fleſh, in a very poor pig which my father
bought of one of his labourers. The pig had
been given very young to the man by my father and was of the ſame litter with ſome we
were then fatting: they were all fed in the
ſame ſtye, and with the ſame food: the *poor* pig
fattened aſtoniſhingly faſt, and was afterwards
found to be as ſuperior in flavour to the others,
as Scarborough mutton is to the large Lincolnſhire or Tees water ſheep.

It

It is fo likewife with fowls, a proof of which
I alfo had. When I lived at Afgafby, in the
vicinity of the Eaft and Weft Fens, the general
opinion of my neighbours was, that a fen-goofe,
from drinking the ftagnant water in the pools,
and living on grafs, would always be found
rank, or at leaft very ftrong, food. I went with
the tide of opinion, and for a long while fan-
cied I had a particular averfion to fen-geefe: but,
the making of experiments might be termed
my hobby-horfe: and, on feeing by accident
thirty fen-geefe, compofed of nothing but fkin
and bone (for they were deftitute of flefh and
feathers), the fituation of the half-ftarved pig
rufhed fo forcibly upon my memory, that I
was induced to buy the whole flock. I put
them in fold amongft fome cattle, where there
was no water to fwim in. What water they
got came from a pump—a very pure fpring.
Their food was barley (for the cattle were fed
on nothing but barley-ftraw); nor could they
get at any thing elfe. After the geefe had remained about a month at this food, I had one
killed and dreffed—a better never was eaten,
and not one of the thirty but was equal to the
firft. There is another prejudice, which fup-

pofes that pulling the feathers whilft alive makes the goofe rank: but thofe I fpeak of, had been pulled thrice at leaft.

It is the quality of the food that determines the tafte of the flefh; this one more inftance may elucidate. Whilft in Lincolnfhire, a man one day at market fold two of the fatteft geefe I had ever feen. My curiofity was ftimulated: I was anxious and inquifitive to know what means were ufed to give them fo great a quantity of flefh and fat. The vender affured me they had eaten nothing but grafs; I thought this muft be a much cheaper method than the one we practifed, which was to give them as many oats almoft as they were worth when killed; and I hoped that from thenceforth I might eat my roaft-geefe, or my goofe-pie, upon cheaper terms than formerly. I had then fome at grafs, which, though not fo fat as thofe the man fold, were yet fatter than any I had fed on corn: but when my goofe came to be put to the fire, I foon refolved upon returning to my old method of feeding with corn; for although this, in common with the reft of my geefe in the field, had as fine a ftream of water as is in any part of England to fwim in, no

fox,

fox, or any other kind of vermin, if put down to roaſt, could ſtink worſe than my graſs-gooſe. She fed on a rich paſture, and ſandy ſoil.

It has been thought by ſome to be very in-different what pigs feed upon, provided they eat and get fat.—A circumſtance that once happened to me may ſerve as a caution to the feeder of pigs, in reſpect of pigs nearly fit for ſlaughtering. I had upwards of forty pigs feed-ing. The gardener pulled up ſome onions, and threw the tops (conſiſting of a barrow-ful) to the pigs. Two days after, I had one of the pigs killed, and in the fry perceived a ſtrong taſte of onions: I had recourſe to the cook for an expla-nation; but ſhe was entirely ignorant of the cauſe. I then applied to the pig-feeder, who readily told me what the gardener had done. The pigs had been confined in a fold, and had no food but ſuch as grains and brewers' waſh. The re-maining part of the pig killed I had ſalted and hung to dry: but it proved to be uneatable, and we threw it away. I mention theſe circum-ſtances, to warn the farmer how neceſſary it is to give ſweet food to ſuch animals as are inten-ded for the table.

But

But to return to fheep. In one refpect they partake of the nature of *oxen:* — I mean that the fmall breed is finer in flefh than the large. A fheep of the Welfh breed, which fhall not weigh more than fix pounds per quarter, will prove of fuperior grain to a Tees-water of fixty pounds per quarter. In like manner, a Scotch bullock of twenty ftone will be finer flefh than one of the Durham or Holdernefs breed of one hundred and twenty ftone: and this rule will hold good in moft animals ufed by us as food.

Having faid fo much on flefh, we fhall now fpeak of the wool, which undoubtedly is fineft on the fmalleft kind of fheep. But the finenefs of the wool is not the certain confequence of a diminutive carcafe: the food is the primary caufe. I have witneffed a fheep from Spain put upon the rich land in Lincolnfhire near Bofton; and in two years this very fheep, the fineft to be procured in Spain, clipped a very unufeful kind of fleece, with more hair than wool. The rich land here referred to is more adapted to the growth of the combing fort of wool, which is the moft valuable of all, as it yields by far the greateft quantity. From four

good

good wethers may be clipped two tods of wool, the wool being frequently fourteen inches long. Allowing, then, one acre of land to keep, during winter and summer, six sheep, we have six stone of wool, which, at one guinea per tod, amounts to 3*l.* 2*s.* 6*d.* But two acres of this land frequently feed a beast likewise: therefore, if a beast pays seventy shillings by feeding for one summer on *two* acres, by allowing thirty-five shillings for one acre, you have an aggregate sum of 7*l.* This kind of land is managed at very little expence: and the profits are great at present. Sheep on the land last-mentioned are better when of a larger size, than those kept in places distant only a few miles from a good market. Sheep of a year old or under cannot bear the fatigue of driving from one to two hundred miles, like those which by age have acquired their full vigour; and the expence of sending a large or small one to market is the same.

The large sort of sheep pay for their food by the great increase in bulk, and will live and thrive on lands improper for fattening cattle and other kinds of sheep. Of such land there are large quantities in the Lincolnshire marshes. And the wool, from situation and for

profit,

profit, is there required to be of a fort fit for combing, and ought to be as nearly as poffible of one length and hair, of an open mellow nature, about ten inches long, even at the top, fo as to have little or no tag; as the tag is not only wafte, but expenfive in cutting off. The food of fheep in thefe marfhes is furprifingly apt to promote the growth of the above fort of wool; and produces it fafter than any other kind of land in England.

When the large fheep feed upon barren foils of a very cold nature, their wool is fettered together and grows into what are called *cots*, and decreafes to half the value of what it would have been in a good rich pafture.

For poor foils, fomething better than moors or mountains, the beft fort of fheep is the Difhley. On fuch foil their wool will be fhorter and weigh lefs; which is occafioned by fuffering hardfhips, and by the want of rich food. The pafture not being fufficient to fatten them; they may be fed with turnips and feeds, which, when good, are excellent for fheep, and caufe them to produce more wool.

Having defcribed the fort of wool moft proper for very good, and for indifferent land, I fhall now fhew what is moft proper for mountains or heaths. The

The fort of wool on sheep feeding in such places ought to be very fine; the finer the better; the length from one to two inches. It must be very thick set: in fact, it cannot be too much so; for the coat preserves the carcass on the bleak unsheltered mountain.

It may now be necessary to remark, that any fort of wool may by attention and management be raised on the same fort of carcass, and on almost all soils; but the nature of the soil will most assuredly in a great degree prevent the wool from attaining the highest perfection. Salt-water land, or land taken from the sea, will produce more wool and of a much heavier nature, and whiter in colour, than any other land whatever.

According to the condition of the sheep in respect to flesh, land sown with grass-seeds, or such as is liable to rot sheep, generally produces white wool. In the latter instance, the whiteness of the wool may be attributed to the great loss of blood the sheep may suffer by flowks in the liver. At Claythorpe, during my four years' residence, I never saw taken out of a sheep fed in that parish one liver free from flowks and eatable.

Sheep

Sheep will fatten on many foils that yet are not congenial to the growth of wool; the wool will be dull, not white and oily, and will weigh light in refpect to the bulk of it.

SECTION XXXII.

The great Ufe of breeding Sheep to fuit different Soils; with Rules drawn from Experience how to breed the Sort required.

IN breeding fheep to fuit different foils there is another confideration to be attended to by the farmer, which is that of ftocking land with fuch a fort as will fuit his fituation in .refpect to diftance from his market. The Difhley fheep fuits almoft all foils, and will profper wherever there is any thing to eat. It has been generally faid, the Difhley fheep did not produce fat lamb, but I have proved the contrary. I had a lamb, got by a Difhley ram out of a Northumberland ewe, that when five months old, weighed twenty pounds per quarter, and altogether fetched forty fhillings. This lamb was killed in the month of September.

Here

Here perhaps I may be told that Mr. Bedel, of Foot's-cray in Kent, very frequently can sell a lamb of less than one third the weight of the one I mention for 3*l.* 3*s.* But we are to consider the different expence of pasture-lamb and house-lamb; and that he confines himself entirely to the breeding of the latter for the London epicures to furnish their tables with at Christmas.

To return to my lamb: Had he had from one to two hundred miles to travel, he would have lost a great deal of weight and value. A two or three years old wether or ewe certainly would not diminish so much by the same journey: but if you can bring a lamb to fetch the value of a two or three years old sheep, the return of money will be quicker, and the profit more considerable.

The large Lincolnshire sheep is proper for some soils. The flesh of this kind of sheep is of a course substance; and though not inclined to feed so quickly as the Dishley, he does not when fat, waste so much in size by travelling to market. His frame is larger, but his flesh not so delicious, or useful to the breeder in respect to value; and there will be found,

U

in

in the fame weight, much more lean and much more bone than in a Difhley fheep. A labourer or hard-working man may prefer a joint of lean rank Lincolnfhire mutton to the Difhley, that will cut from five to fix inches deep of firm fat; but he will not find an equal weight of it fatisfy fo many hungry children as the Difhley fat mutton. Without doubt there exifts a very confiderable difference amongft that fpecies we term Lincolnfhire fheep. Some of them, when driven the diftance of one hundred miles from their native paftures, appear to be little better than carrion: but if thofe fheep, when intended to be kept until they were three years or three and a half old, or at leaft till they were three times clipped, had a little more attention beftowed with judgment upon them, they would be found to produce more wool, and retain their flefh much better.

The Wiltfhire fheep and the Hertfordfhire fheep I do not treat of, being no judge of them. They are chiefly for folding: and the folding of fheep I do not like; it is robbing Peter to pay Paul.

Of

Of the tall slender sheep from the mountains, some will thrive and fatten on a rich soil with luxuriant pasture; others are not to be made fat by any means.

The square short-legged breed from the forests or downs, will live on barren land, and bite the closest of any; and with good keep they will soon be fit for the butcher, but not very fat.

I am of opinion, all sheep, according to their first value, might be improved equal to the Dishley or long-woolled sheep. The Downs sheep are the most useful and profitable next to the Dishley; and had as much attention been paid to them by a set of men equally capable as the breeders of the Leicestershire sheep, they might have been brought to equal perfection. They appear to be equally profitable on some soils capable of producing carding-wool. They are good-fleshed sheep, and will bear more hardships on dry land than any long-woolled sheep. They are naturally active, and some of them quick feeders. There are some of the Welsh sheep very useful. These sort of short-woolled sheep would never be made profitable in the Licolnshire marshes.

The

The Norfolk sheep are of a great size, and sometimes profitable: but perhaps few sheep are better kept; their winter food being superior to that of any other country, and their layer continually dry. No sheep likes or will prosper on wet land. The fort called Lincolnshire-sheep do the best upon such land.

SECTION XXXIII.

The cheapest and most expeditious Method of feeding sheep.

THE cheapest and most expeditious method of feeding sheep in the winter, is to give them rape, cole, or turnips, in penns or trays, as explained in Section XII. p. 59.

Rape and cole should be eaten in the same way as the turnips. The folding in a straw-fold would doubtless save hundreds of sheep which die of the refp or red-water. The losses sustained in the Lincolnshire fens are innumerable for want of such caution. See Section XXXIV.

The

The cheapeſt food in ſummer upon good land is graſs, although not the moſt fattening. Good ſeeds fatten them quicker upon moderately good ſoils, ſuch as do not carry more ſheep than can thereon do well ; for it often happens that upon too luxuriant land ſheep thrive but indifferently, by their being ſuch numbers feeding on it until it actually ſtinks of them.

Great advantage would ariſe from feeding ſheep in the ſummer on green food, in the ſame manner as is deſcribed for horſes, beaſts, &c. Green tares and cabbages, &c. would be very quick-fattening and cheap food.

SECTION XXXIV.

Diſorders incident to Sheep; with the Methods of Cure.

ONE of the moſt extraordinary diſorders to which ſheep are liable is called the *red-water* or *reſp.* This diſeaſe undoubtedly is brought on by the ſtomach and bowels being overloaded with food too much abounding with juices.

Turnips

Turnips will give it to sheep, as likewise will rape or cole; so will eddish, young clover, or any kind of grass where rich manure has recently been laid on the land.

I had twelve acres of clover, with one hundred ewes and lambs upon it. I intended to sow the field with turnips; but, the weather being dry, I could not plough it. In order to be ready against wet weather came, I had the manure carried on the land. A twenty-four hours' rain fell; and the next day three ewes were dead with the *red-water*, though both ewes and lambs had been constantly there for some weeks without a single accident. It may be necessary to observe that the manure was taken out of the fold-yard, and consisted chiefly of rich horse-dung, cow-dung, pig-dung, &c. It was laid in heaps, so that, when the rain came, the furrows ran with a black-coloured water, the juices of the manure. Since this accident I have heard and known of many similar, and from the same cause. I caution the farmer against putting sheep upon land newly manured, especially if with fresh dung: it makes the plants to be over succulent for the animals' bowels.

To

To cure the *red-water*, the beſt remedy I know is ſoot from pit-coal, mixt up with ſalt water, or with ſalt and chamberlye. Mix ſo much ſalt with water that an egg will ſwim; and put for every ſheep a large ſpoonful of ſoot: ſtir the ingredients well together, and let them remain until the following day, or about twelve hours. Give three large ſpoonfuls for a doſe to each ſheep early in the morning, after it has been kept from food the preceding night. Repeat the above doſe every fifth or ſixth day, if the ſheep are much affected by the diſorder, and you will find the medicine an effectual remedy. I hardly ever knew it fail of working a perfect cure.

Raiſing the ſheep at night, and driving them about ſo as to cauſe them to empty themſelves, is another good and ſimple remedy; for a ſheep, being a greedy animal, fills his ſtomach with food; and, being naturally indolent, he lies a conſiderable time in one poſture, which prevents a proper digeſtion, which moderate exerciſe would effectually promote. It is not uncommon for the coats of the ſtomachs to be ſo diſtended as to burſt ſome of the many ſanguiferous veſſels with which they ſo amply abound,

bound, and whofe ufe is to fecret the liquor gaftricus, or liquor of the ftomachs. By an accident of this kind I have had fheep die fuddenly; and have upon a clofe examination into the caufe of their death, taken from two to three gallons of red-water from the infide of one fheep. The bowels were full of this water, which feemed tinged with blood, and emitted a very putrid fmell. Part of the flefh was in a mortified ftate, and ftunk horridly, which it will do even before life has left the fheep.

The above prefcription will not fail of ridding the animal of this terrible diforder. The firft object is to cleanfe the bowels, and brace the ftomach: the falt does the one, and the foot, I fuppofe, the other. This diforder feldom happens in the fummer, unlefs to a fheep who gets over-caft; for a fheep does not lie ftill in fummer above four hours in the four-and-twenty: but in winter he lies ftill full half the time, that is, twelve hours out of the twenty-four.

This diforder may be totally prevented by following the method before laid down for fattening fheep with turnips or cole, that is, by moving them into the ftraw-fold at night. Do this early in the evening; and you may eafily

raife

raife them before you go to bed and with little trouble give them the quantity of exercife which may be thought neceffary. The giving of frefh folds of turnips in the evening frequently brings on this diforder, and occafions almoft immediate death, efpecially if the fheep have been kept rather fhort of food for fome days before. I have known fifty fheep in one hundred die of it in the courfe of one winter. If by adminiftering the medicine here recommended, and by ufing the ftraw-fold, five only of the fifty had been faved, it would well have paid the trouble attending their cure.

It is very neceffary that fheep fhould be carefully attended, that, on the firft fymptoms of the above or any other diftemper, remedies may be applied, and a cure attempted in time.

There is a diforder in fheep called the *turn* or *giddy*. This diforder proceeds from a bleb of watery matters formed upon the brain. Some people attempt a cure by opening or trepanning the fkull, extracting the bleb, and then clofing the parts again: but this operation, however eafy to an expert furgeon, is too difficult and dangerous to fucceed in the hands of fuch clumfy operators as are generally employed on fuch occafions: and fix out of feven of

the patients die under their hands. I have
cured great numbers of this diforder by a very
eafy and fimple method. I take the fheep
by the ears, which I pull violently, and then
cut off as clofe as poffible to the head : this is
the beft remedy I ever tried; and the trial is
never attended with danger. I do not pretend
to explain how this effects a cure : it is fufficient
for me to affert the fact. Perhaps the violent
pulling of the ears may difturb the collection
of watery matter ; and the cutting them clofe
to the head may give vent to it by the hæ-
morrhage which follows of courfe. Whatever
may be the caufe, the remedy is pretty fure.

It was by accident I difcovered this more
perfect cure for the *giddy*. When I lived with
my father, one of our lamb-hogs had taken
the *turn*. I ordered the fhepherd to catch it,
that I might cut off the ears. When fheep
have this diforder, they will frequently turn
round for a long time together, have a ftupid
heavy look, quit their companions and feed
by themfelves. You may go very near them
before they difcover you; which feems to indicate that they lofe their hearing. But as foon
as they become fenfible of your approach, they
will

will run as fwift as they did before the diforder feized them. The fhepherd went behind to catch it : but the moment the lamb perceived him, it ran away, and continued running for about ten minutes. It was an excellent chace, and afforded fine fport, which I relifhed highly. The fhepherd, who was a famous runner, was terribly enraged againft the poor lamb ; and, as foon as he overtook it, began to pull and twirl it moft violently round by the ears. As it was at a confiderable diftance when he caught it, he had full time to gratify his revenge. I immediately cut off the ears, and in two days the lamb was perfectly cured.

I had fucceeded pretty well before the time now fpoken of, in curing the diftemper by only cutting off the ears : but repeated prac- tice has proved to me in the moft fatisfactory manner, that pulling the ears violently before they are cut off is the beft method of enfuring the cure : you may depend upon faving nine out of ten, at leaft. I have never known this diforder to return after having been once cured.

Thofe ewes which have or have had this dif- order are no worfe for breeding, as the lambs do not take the diforder from their dams. The

The *foot-rot* is a difeafe which will attack numbers at the fame time. Sheep, when feeding on a hot fandy foil, are very liable to contract it, from the particles of fand or gravel getting into their feet; as likewife in wet weather, when the grafs is long. If one fingle fheep fhould be attacked by the diforder, it would be advifeable to feparate him immediately from the reft at the time of folding; for, if the fhepherd does not ufe fuch precaution, he may expect a great part of the flock to be infected by the fheep treading on each other's feet. I had from a gentleman a ram who had the foot-rot, and I was fo negligent as to put him in the month of September, with fifty ewes, upon land where I never knew fheep to be troubled with the difeafe; nor had the ewes been affected before. I had before known that it was contagious, or what fhepherds call *fmitting*, though I did not fuppofe it was fo dangerous. I thought the worft confequence that poffibly could enfue would be the giving me a little trouble: and I am fond of trying experiments. A great number of the ewes caught the diforder: nor could I get them entirely clear the whole year; although I attended

them

them clofely myfelf during the progrefs of their cure. However valuable a tup might be, I would not accept of him as a gift for the purpofe of going with ewes, were he troubled with the foot-rot, unlefs I cured him firft.

The method of cure is as follows: Pare the foot with great care, fo as not to injure the quick : look narrowly for the gravel, which is often fo much inclofed that it is difficult to extract it ; and when that happens, the animal will fuffer great pain, and fpeedily decreafe in flefh. Where the gravel is, the hoof will be very hard, hot, and dry. In paring the foot, you muft be careful not to cut fo much as to make it bleed; for that will retard the cure. Take blue vitriol ; pound it very fine, and apply it to the part affected. Some ufe for this purpofe the blue vitriol-water, which is eafily procured at the chemifts' or apothecaries' fhops, and is made by diffolving three ounces of blue vitriol, and two ounces of alum, in a pint and a half of vinegar; and afterwards adding two ounces of ftrong fpirit or oil of vitriol, and letting it ftand for ufe. Some ufe with fuccefs, clear fpirits or oil of vitriol alone : but, from the violence of this remedy, it muft

be

uſed with the greateſt caution. Any ſtrong
aſtringent, ſuch as aquafortis, &c. may like-
wiſe be applied with advantage.

Much rain will, no doubt, frequently occaſion this diſtemper, eſpecially if the paſture
be of a hot burning nature, and the graſs long
and luxuriant. The long continued wet opens
the pores of the feet and cauſes them to ſwell:
and, on the return of the hot weather, they
are ſuddenly contracted, and incloſe ſand and
other noxious matters. Indeed what we call
by the general term of *foot-rot* differs widely
in reſpect to cauſes or ſymptoms; and each
variety of the diſeaſe requires a different treatment. In ſome caſes, on examining the ſheep's
foot, you will find it much inflamed between
the claws, and a ſubſtance ſomething ſimilar to
wax incloſed in little bags. To cure this, get
a ſmall hook made of ſtrong iron-wire, with a
handle; put the hook in the hole which you
will find formed by nature: take faſt hold of
the ſkin, and pull it towards you, ſo that you
may, with a ſharp knife, cut round the hook
and take the bleb or matter clean out. Dreſs
the wounds by applying tar with about one
ſixth part of verdegris, and a little ſalt, well
mixed

mixed together. Take care to rub this com-
pofition in between the claws, and it will
effect a cure.

The *scab* is a diforder in fheep which is eafily
cured. It is a cutaneous difeafe, fomething
like the itch amongft men. If it be of a mild
fort, and the cure be attempted in time, to-
bacco-water (or river-water ftrongly impregnated by fteeping tobacco in it) will remove it,
without rifk ; for, as this lotion is perfectly ino-
fenfive, the fheep may be wafhed with it without much danger.

If the difeafe is of the more virulent kind,
the cure is performed by an application of the
common blue ointment of the fhops, which is
compofed of quickfilver and hog's-lard, in the
proportion of two ounces of quickfilver to
fixteen ounces of the lard ; and may be had,
ready made for ufe, at any chemift, druggift,
or apothecary's, as there is generally a large
demand for this ointment for other purpofes
than that of curing the fcab in fheep. A pound
of the ointment will be fufficient for four
fheep. It is very neceffary that the greateft
caution fhould be ufed in applying this ointment, moft efpecially if ewes have lambs
fucking

fucking them: the fucking their mothers and hot weather will bring on or occasion salivation, and prove fatal to the lambs. A friend of mine once had a very heavy loss on salving his ewes at clipping day.

My method is, to lay on the ointment in very small quantities, in sheds four inches asunder, and to rub it into the skin as perfectly as possible.

This ointment in clumsy injudicious hands kills many sheep in hot weather: but I do my sheep lightly over with it at the latter end of every season, at an expence of two-pence per head, to destroy fags and lice. It is a great preserver of wool, whereas mercury-water is apt to clot and spoil it.

There are disorders which are called the *meagrims*, *rickets*, and *rubbers*. These diseases are supposed by many to arise from breeding from the same sort of sheep a long time together on the same land: but this opinion was fully confuted by Mr. Bakewell; for he persevered in breeding from one sort of sheep on the same soil, for a considerable number of successive years, without any inconvenience of the kind.

However

However, when fheep are once infected, it is certain that, if the farmer will then perfift in breeding from the tainted ftock, he will run the rifque of lofing his whole flock; for thefe difeafes are undoubtedly hereditary. I therefore advife the farmer, fo foon as he perceives the diftemper gaining ground, to change the breed; as no perfect cure has ever, to my knowledge, been performed by any means hitherto employed.

When a fheep is attacked by the *meagrims,* the fymptoms are, cocking his tail like a well-nicked horfe: he will canter like a lady's pad; and if you clap your hand upon his back, he will immediately drop down; which feems to indicate that the diforder is feated in the back of the animal. *Rickets* are fo much like mea-grims, that I have never been able to dif-tinguifh the one from the other.

When a fheep has the *rubbers,* it occafions fuch an itching that, if he can get near a poft, a tree, or any thing proper for his purpofe, he will rub himfelf to death—he will neglect his food and fall into a regular decline, and be two or three months dying.

Heavy

Heavy loffes have been fuftained from the havoc made by the above diforders, which fhould be carefully guarded againft.

When a fheep is attacked by the diforder called the *black-leg*; if he be fat, the fooner you kill him the better; I never knew one cured. You will firft perceive a black fpot near the ftifle joint, and the fheep will become fo lame as fcarcely to be able to move: this fpot generally increafes very rapidly, and foon turns to a mortification. I have tried fomentations and many other remedies; but all in vain. I muft own that I have never heard a rational explanation given of the caufe of this diforder; nor can I account for it. I have fometimes been tempted to attribute the appearance of the diforder to fome external injury by a blow: but on reflection I have dropped that opinion: for it cannot be a bruife. It is more probable that it is caufed by the bite of fome venomous reptile, as it often happens that a number of fheep have it in the fame pafture.

Blindnefs in fheep is a very common difeafe, and is brought on by a cold falling into the eyes. The moft difagreeable confequence enfuing from it is the danger of the fheep's drowning himfelf, himself, if there should be a pond or other receptacle for water in the pasture.

What will cure blindness in one animal, will no doubt be good for the eyes of another. I make an ointment with honey and verdigris, called distilled verdigris, finely pounded. I dip a duck's feather in the ointment, and gently apply it to the eye. The feather you make use of cannot be too soft: or, if a skin be formed on the eye, you may put a little of the verdigris into a quill, and blow it on the eye. This disorder will cure of itself, if let alone; but will cause the carcass of the sheep to shrink very much.

The *white skit*, in sucking lambs, is cured by a table spoonful of runnet or yearning put into about half a pint of milk just taken from the cow, and given immediately; that is, before the milk has time to turn into perfect curds and whey, as the cure depends upon the milk getting into the rumen or first stomach before it becomes completely turned. This disorder is the effect of a cold, and generally seizes the lamb about the time he begins to eat plentifully of grass, and to suck less milk.

The

The *green-skit* is another diforder in lambs.
If you put a green willow round its neck, it
will effect a cure.

To deftroy *maukes* in fheep, take two ounces
of mercury fublimate pounded, one pint of
fpirits of turpentine, and one gallon of water :
mix the whole well together, and fhake it up
every time you ufe it. It is a good way to wafh
the wool affected in clean water after the
maukes are taken out : and, if they have
penetrated the fkin, rub on the part a little
tar, to prevent the mercury from doing injury. After the wool is wafhed, you muft
apply fome more worm-water, or the flies will
ftrike the part again.

For *fly-beating*, or *galling*, the part muft
be covered by fome means with cloth ; and
it is proper to hopple the fheep behind, if
it be upon his head, to prevent his fcratch-
ing. The hoppling will not prevent his thriving.

SECTION

SECTION XXXV.

The proper Time for putting the Ram to the Ewes; with the Method of treating the Ewes when Lambing.

THE beſt time for putting the ram to the ewes is about the tenth of October: if for early fat lambs, the beginning of September, when they have only graſs to feed on. The ſpace of five weeks is a ſufficient time for the ram to remain with the ewes

When ewes ſeem ready to yean their lambs, great caution ſhould be uſed by the ſhepherd. He ſhould not be over-forward in giving them aſſiſtance, but ſuffer nature to complete her work. Much damage has ariſen from impatience or haſtineſs of temper on ſuch occaſions: I therefore recommend the waiting with coolneſs the proper time. Circumſtances ſometimes ariſe, where help may be neceſſary, but nature will act ſufficiently her own part ninety-nine times in the hundred.

If an ewe gives ill from lambing, I always found ſpirits of turpentine applied to the part, and good nurſing with caudles, &c. to be the beſt remedies. SECTION

SECTION XXXVI.

Sheep-Shearing: Reasons why the Time should vary according to Situation.

IN situations near woods, which common-ly abound with flies, those galling enemies to new-shorn sheep, they should be clipped the beginning of June.

But in open countries, downs, or marshes it is advisable to clip late; for there they will not be much in danger of being galled by those flies which so cruelly infest them near woods or thick hedges; and as great part of the sheep may be intended to be made fat and sold that season, by clipping late you obtain a greater quantity of wool. The hot weather occasions wool to grow fast from the free circulation of the natural oil; and July, in my opinion, will be early enough to commence shearing in the last-mentioned situations.

SECTION

SECTION XXXVII.

Method of treating Sheep before Shearing, by Washing the Wool: Reasons why they should go a certain Time in the Wool between Washing and Shearing.

SHEEP should be washed ten days at least, and not more than fourteen days before clipping. the sheep are not suffered to rest at least ten days between the washing and clipping of them, the wool will not have recovered the natural oil which has been expelled or squeezed out together with the filth in washing; and it will be dry and hask. Although the wool, if clipped wet, would, when first taken from the sheep, weigh more than if clipped dry; yet, after keeping it a little, you will find it considerably lighter than what has been taken off the sheep dry. A fleece shorn wet will soon diminish in weight: one taken off dry will not. The reason is obvious—The water which the wool imbibes by washing, soon evaporates; water being an heterogeneous intruder, and soon expelled; whilst oil, one of the component principles of wool, obstinately retains its natural situation.   If

If you fuffer fheep to go longer than four-teen days between wafhing and clipping, the wool will be liable to receive injury by dirt or filth; which will diminifh the value, though it may add to the immediate weight. It will be of advantage to houfe the fheep the night be-fore clipping; they will then fweat much, and rub againft each other; which will not only add weight to the wool, but alfo foften it, give it a finer appearance, and abfolutely render it bet-ter. However fome men may defpife thefe *niceties* (as they may term them), they will find their account by practifing them.

Provide yourfelf with a bottle of fpirits of turpentine; and if the fhearer fnip the fkin in fhearing, twift a bit of wool round a ftick, which dip in the bottle, and dab on the wound. Apply then a fmall quantity of tar to the part, which will keep off the flies, and turn the rain. The lambs, four or five days after their mo-thers are clipped, will be found to have the fags and lice. Thefe vermine may be deftroyed by a lotion compofed of arfenic mixed up with water and foft foap. The following is a re-cipe for making the lotion: Two pounds of ar-fenic boiled in a fmall quantity of water, which after-

afterwards may be increafed to the quantity of twenty gallons by adding fo much more water. In this mixture diffolve two pounds of foft foap: you then will have ftuff fufficient to wafh a number of lambs. The readieft method is to put it in a tube large enough to contain a lamb: and the fhepherd muft have an affiftant; for one perfon muft lay hold of the fore legs of the lamb, and with the other hand take hold of the crown of the head; as the head muft on no account be immerfed in the wafh, fince fwallowing a very fmall portion would inevitably poifon the lamb. Let the affiftant take hold of the hind legs, and in this manner dip the lamb, which need not remain longer in the tub than is fufficient to wet his wool. An empty tub muft be at hand, to let the lamb ftand in to drain the water from the wool, or he would carry away a great quantity of fuperfluous water with him. When the lamb is placed in the tub to drain, the men muft with their hands wring the wool, to force out the wet. The tub laft mentioned muft be frequently emptied.

SECTION XXXVIII.

Description of a Ram proper to get the best Stock.

THOSE who wish to reap great profit by breeding, should bestow a particular attention in the choice of a ram : for by a good choice their wish is most likely to be gratified ; by a bad choice, they at best are sure to receive little emolument, and perhaps may suffer great loss.

The male animal communicates his good or bad qualities to his offspring. To prove this, I have tried many experiments with swine and dogs. By putting to a long-eared sow, first a long-eared lean boar of the same kind, and then a tunky short-eared one, I have procured at the same litter two species of pigs, which, though all suckled together and kept alike, ever after remained dissimilar and distinct : those by the short-eared boar fattened with as little keep as I ever saw : the others by the long-eared sire were lean, and could not

be

be made fat without a very large quantity of food.

Respecting the produce of the above sow, it proves that when a sow is brimmed by one boar, if you send her to another, she will in all probability have more pigs. This sow had twelve pigs, ten long-eared white ones, and two tunky black ones. The sow was white and long-eared; the boar the same. The tunky boar was black. A man who has but one sow, and is desirous to have some roasting pigs, some of a small kind for pork, and some of a large kind for profit, may in all probability have them at the same litter. As a sow gives more milk the first month than afterwards; it would do well to kill a few pigs off at the expiration of that time: the sow would rear the remainder better, and at less expence. And if two sows are kept instead of one, the roasting-pigs would nearly be clear gain.

With grey-hounds I have made similar trials. A very middling bitch, if put to a capital dog, breeds a good-running dog: but put the best bitch to a bad-running dog, the whelps will be good for little or nothing. It is my

opinion,

opinion, that race-horfes are the eafieft to breed of any, as the male and female are fo fufficiently tried that they cannot vary much. There are no general rules without exceptions ; but fewer in the following than any—" Like " get like."

To choofe a proper ram, it will be of advantage to keep in mind what has already been faid in defcribing the beft fort of fheep, and to remember the Difhley, new Leicefter or Bakewell ram: all fheep, whether you breed them large or fmall, for foreft or pafture, ought to be of that make.

His back or upper part fhould be like the top part of a tortoife ; his head fmall, and his back broad. He fhould be broad in his breaft, round in his ribs, wide in his hind quarters, let down low in his twift. His tail fhould ftand low ; fo that the fat of his cufhion will defcend farther down into his leg towards the fhank. His bone muft be fmall, his eye quick. As to fize, every one muft judge for himfelf, and feledt him according to the purpofe he may want him for. I recommend to keep a fheep within fome moderate compafs ; for when you make an attempt for a larger fize,

you

you will get more bone, and inevitably lofe fo much fat or thrift; and, as you will lofe it gradually, you may go too far in increafing the bulk of your fheep, before you perceive it : and thrift in all animals intended to be fattened, is the object which fhould be moft carefully attended to.

Let the fort of wool be according to the intended fituation; for I am of opinion, that every fort of wool may be grown on one fort of flefh; and there are good and bad-flefhed animals of all defcriptions.

Rams of different ages have been recommended by many different perfons: I have tried them from one year to ten years old, and never found any material difference in the ftock in refpect to quality; but in quantity I certainly have. It may eafily be fuppofed that a ram two or three years old will get more ftock than one ten years old. The proper number of ewes for a fhearling ram is from fifty to fixty. I have turned a two-fhear ram to nine fcore of ewes, and of that number only five miffed. I had that tup from Mr. Chaplin; my men called him the Grand Seignor: but I queftion whether his

Sublime

Sublime Highnefs made fuch effectual ufe of his feraglio.

After all, I muft own that I do not approve of any ram being put with more than fix fcore of ewes: it is, in my opinion, as many as any one ought to have. If he is a valuable ram, he fhould be allowed a *teazer*, fufficiently fecured to prevent mifchief, and the ewes fhould be put to him in a proper place.

SECTION XXXIX.

Foreſt Sheep, and the Improvement that Kind are capable of.

FOREST fheep fhould not intermix fo as to crofs the breed, but be kept to their own kind; for many reafons—their wonderful agility in leaping from rock to rock, their activity and fpeed in fearch of food, that wonderful inftinct they are endowed with by nature, in lying down in fuch places as the fnow fhall not drift over them: a caution fo abfolutely necef-fary to fheep in mountainous parts. The Difhley fheep are the reverfe of the foreft fort; for though the Difhley with great care and good food are fo very profitable, yet are they

the

the most tender sheep I ever knew. They are starved if the least neglected : they soon become fat in good keep, but poor with indifferent.

If you choose to cross the breed of forest sheep with the Dishley, draw a few of the best into an inclosed pasture, and put your favourite ram to them. This will be found the surest and best method to improve them ; but I do not think it would answer to stock the mountains with sheep so bred: they would require more care and attention than could be there given them.

SECTION XL.

Description of Fold-yards : Necessity of a Receptacle for the Juices which drain from the Fold-yard; and the best method of applying the same.

THE fold-yard ought to be so situated amongst the buildings, as easily to receive every sort of manure: which the pigs by routing and turning it over continually will thoroughly intermix. The cattle will eat much of the litter which is thrown out from the

horse-horfe-ftables, which always contains fmall quantities of hay wafted by the horfes, and at times a little corn and other matters, which by this management will turn to the farmer's profit in a greater degree than if the fame quantity of fuch hay had been taken from the ftack, and immediately fpread in the fold-yard; as the cattle in this cafe eat a great deal of the horfe-dung or refufe ftraw along with it. The fold-yard fhould be nearly level, with a fmall inclination or flope towards the receptacle or refervoir.

I cannot approve of the management of thofe who would give the fold-yard the form of the infide of a bowl: in fuch a concavity, the cattle on the approach of winter would ftarve by lying fo much in wet: neither would the manure be fo foon fit for ufe; for the materials it is compofed of, if conftantly covered with water, would fcarcely ever rot. Any man may fatisfy himfelf of the truth of this affertion, by immerfing manure in water and keeping it conftantly covered.—A fingular proof of this happened not many years fince in the vicinity of London. In finking a well at Tottenham Court, on the eftate of the late

lord

lord Southampton, at about eighteen feet from the furface the workmen dug into fomething foft, which, upon being fent up in the bucket, was found to contain the paunch or *rumen* of an animal, with a quantity of undigefted hay, to all appearance as if it had been chewed but a few hours before. On further fearch, the horns of the cow and part of the head with the hair on, were feparated by the axe and fpade. Incredible as it may feem, the whole appeared as frefh as if they had been recently depofited; though afterwards proved to have lain there upwards of forty years. Upon enquiry, it was difcovered that the identical fpot had been a large pit, or pond of water, into which at the time of the great diftemper amongft the horned cattle a neighbouring cowkeeper, who then rented the place, had thrown a great number of cows which had died of it. The pond afterwards was filled up, chiefly by rubbifh from London; and it is almoft unneceffary to add, that the prefent proprietor immediately had the well clofed again.

The fold-yard, then, fhould have a fmall declination or flope from where the rain falls from the buildings, and in general from every

other part of the premisses, so that the refuse
of the house, and all other washings, may
gently ooze into the reservoir or common receptacle. If the fold-yard is paved, one inch drip
in twelve feet will be found to be sufficient.

The reservoir must be made sufficiently ca-
pacious and deep enough to receive a quantity
of roots, corn-stubble, earth from different
soils, &c. which will imbibe the juices as
they gradually ooze in, and form a matter that,
when taken out, will ferment strongly, and in
this manner be worked into a good compost
very little inferior to the fold-manure. By
using this compost (as prescribed in the Method of making Fallows) at the latter end of
the year, or so soon as harvest is over, the
farmer will reap more benefit than at first he
will think possible. He will raise a dunghill
from the greatest nuisances; for what can be
more injurious to land than the roots of stubble, which, like wood, rob the soil of nourishment, and keep the parts from adhering sufficiently close to assist vegetation in the ensuing
crop.

It is not enough to make the reservoir
sufficiently large: the bottom of it must be
well

well rammed in with ftiff clay to fuch a thicknefs as to retain the juices, and not fuffer the
fine parts to drain away. The liquor or juice
retained in the refervoir too foon and readily
evaporates, and is loft when thrown on the
land in its natural ftate. The farmer therefore
will be careful to have all the parts well
worked together into one body, as directed
above.

SECTION XLI.

*Reafons why Stall-feeding in Summer ought to
be practifed, from Tares, Clover-grafs, Cab-
bage, &c.*

STALL-FEEDING horfes for the plough,
&c. has already been recommended in Section
XIV. p. 97; where I mentioned the ufes of
clover: but fold-feeding cattle, pigs, foals, in
fummer, and fome other circumftances were
not fufficiently noticed. From ftall-feeding
in fummer the farmer may derive great affiftance towards improving his land; as abundance
of the beft kind of manure may be made by

cattle

cattle of all kinds eating green fodder in folds, or ftalls: and I am firmly of opinion that beafts intended for the flaughter-houfe will fatten much quicker by ftall-feeding; as, in the heat of fummer, the flies difturb their reft, make them uneafy, and occafion them to run about continually; which muft prevent their becoming fat.

Hunters and race-horfes would, from the quantity of meat they eat, be as fat as pigs, if exercife did not keep them down. It would be fingular to fee an Irifh labourer, accuftomed daily to run up and down a ladder four ftories high, over-loaded with flefh : a fat alderman is not a very great curiofity. Therefore, were cattle tied up, and fuffered to enjoy reft, by eating their food in peace, they would feed more heartily, and the mown food would not be liable to be fpoiled by dunging or ftalling upon it ; which muft happen to a confiderable part when cattle feed in the field.

Red-clover, if intended for horfes to feed upon, fhould be brought into the fold-yard or ftable; as animals of weight by treading upon a plant of fuch a pulpy nature will fpoil much more than they eat. To be convinced of this,

let

let the *old* farmer put four horfes upon an acre
of clover to depafture it, and let him keep an
account of the number of days the piece keeps
the four horfes. Then let him keep the fame
number of horfes in the ftable, and feed them
with the clover mown from a field of the
fame extent. He will find the horfes which
have depaftured to have deftroyed three times
as much with their feet as with their mouths
—befides the lofs of that manure which they
would have made by being fed in the ftall or
fold.

We will now confider the objections commonly made againft ftall-feeding. The firft
will be, that clover is not fit to cut fo early
as it is to depafture. The fecond objection is
the trouble of cutting and fetching it home.
The firft objection I allow—it is a real inconvenience ; as the month's keeping in May is
of great value : but if we, the preceding year,
make into hay a proportion fufficient for that
month or until the clover gets ftrong enough
to mow, the difficulty is got over.

To the fecond objection I fay, that the
trouble of fetching home the clover is little
more than that of driving the horfes to and from
the

the clofe where it grows: and if you feed them in the fold, you will not be under the neceffity of fetching them a mile or two when you rife to your labour in the morning, nor of taking them the fame diftance in the evening.

I have frequently mentioned cutting wheat-ftraw with the clover; and I do moft earneft-ly recommend the practice with every kind of green food for the reafons already ftated, and on account of the great faving which the farmer will find by the ufe. I likewife advife to give the horfes which eat green food their corn late in the evening: the laft thing you do before you go to bed. If you give it in the morning, and then immediately go to work, the corn quickly paffes without contributing to their fupport by proper digeftion.

From the refufe of the green fodder, with a fmall addition of other food, a number of pigs may be kept; and they would increafe the ma-nure-hill.

In refpect to foals, they might not poffibly do fo well with this management: but if they are put in the ftall for the day, and well fed and let out for the night in fome pafture, they would add to the dunghill, and thrive much

better

better than if (as they frequently are) either
ftanding in a pond of water the whole day, or
under fome tree, ftamping their manure, to
no ufe. If they drop it in the pond, it is totally loft. Let the farmer calculate the damage done to grafs by cattle trampling upon
and brufing the very roots, and he will foon
give the preference to ftall-feeding.

Feeding with cabbages is rather a new plan,
but I am of opinion it will foon be generally
practifed. They afford abundance of good
food in fummer : and, as they may be cut two
or three times, great profit muft undoubtedly
arife from the ufe of them. The expence of raifing cabbages is not great.

SECTION XLII.

Ufe of a Fold in Winter to turn Stall-fed Cattle in.

STALL-FED cattle without doubt would
thrive better to have their liberty a few hours
in the middle of the day; for by continually
ftanding in one pofture the animals are prevented from indulging themfelves, and rub-

bing

bing their hides, in which they take particular delight; they feel uncomfortable and cannot fleep eafy, and this will prevent their feeding freely. Conftantly breathing in the fame crib or trough makes the place unpleafant to the beafts: a free uncontaminated air is as necef-fary to them as to men.

Moft of us know what effect foul air has upon the human frame, and but few are igno-rant of the bad and often fatal confequences of it to cattle: their breath, however naturally fweet, may become very ftrong from the na-ture of the food they take, fuch as turnips, cabbages, linfeed-cakes, &c. which, without a fufficient circulation of air, will fill the whole place with a putrid fteam highly noxious to beafts and man.

I obferved the cow-keepers in the vicinity of London, who in general keep a very great number, make it a conftant practice to turn their cows after milking into a cold and dirty layer, or fold as we call it. Being a brewer, and keeping cows myfelf, which were fed near-ly as thofe in the neighbourhood of London are, I tried the method, and was foon convinced of the utility of it. For, having made particular

ular inquiries of the fervant who fed my cows, I learnt that feveral at one time feemed to loathe their food, that in general they did not appear to have very good appetites, and that fome would not eat their grains for fome days together. On my adopting the cuftom of turning them out for fix hours in the day-time, the cows foon began to appear healthy and to fatten apace, and were never off their appetite.

With grains mixed with cut ftraw I have fed cows to be very good beef; and have milked them to the day on which they were killed.

I have found it an excellent method to give chopped ftraw to beafts with all kinds of rich food; as it is more pleafant to their palates, makes them ruminate more, promotes a regular digeftion, and prevents the too quick paffing of the moift or juicy food through the inteftines.

Bb   SECTION

SECTION XLIII.

Method of treating Horses for Husbandry in Winter, on a much better and cheaper Plan than is usually practised.

HERE again cut ſtraw will be found of infinite uſe, and ſave many loads of hay. Although hay, in ſome parts of the kingdom diſtant from a market, may not be frequently offered for ſale, and conſequently the farmer not ſet ſo high a value upon it; yet if he kept a regular account of what hay is eaten by his horſes during the winter, and charged the coſt and trouble of making and harveſting it, and the rent of the land, he would find them a ſerious and heavy expence; as will be more fully explained in Section XLVI.

I am of opinion, that in London, where hay is generally dear, it is the moſt expenſive thing to feed a horſe with. I knew a ſtable-keeper of eminence, who was of the ſame opinion: he always ſaid hay was dearer than corn; and as he dealt largely in both, he was likely to know ſomething of the matter. I have always found it to be ſo.

I have

I have tried experiments to keep horſes upon grains, potatoes, ground corn, bran, malt-combs, carrots, &c.; but never found any thing ſo cheap as chopped ſtraw. During the winter 1795 and 1796, I did not ſuffer one of the nine horſes I kept for the uſe of my brewery to eat any hay whatever. I kept two ſaddle-hor-ſes, which at times were ridden hard, and were never free from fair work (for I do not like man or beaſt to be idle); the principal part of their food was likewiſe chopped ſtraw, with a regular quantity of corn. I ſet apart for this purpoſe the produce of ſix acres of wheat *ſcouge*, or wheat ſtraw laſhed. I ſet a man to thraſh ſome of the ſtraw over again, by way of ſeeing how much wheat would be conſumed in the ſtraw. He was two days on this buſineſs: but the wheat he got out was worth no more than the coſt of three day's labour. I muſt alſo ac-knowledge that the wheat in this ſtraw had a great deal of the fuzzball or ſmut, and for that reaſon was not thraſhed, but *laſhed*, left the flail ſhould bruiſe the fuzzballs, and turn all the wheat black. Wheat at the time was eight ſhillings per buſhel. I therefore ſaved the wheat-ſtraw, and added ſix acres of Tartarian oats, which were remarkably long, ſix feet up-

on

on an average. This quantity of oats and wheat-fcouge ferved my nine horfes from the middle of September 1795, to the month of June 1796, without any rack-meat or grafs. In the month of June the nine draught horfes were turned out to grafs, during night.

It is to be obferved here, that I do not fpeak of chopped ftraw as a fubftitute for corn : but I mean that it may well fupply the place of hay; and in fuch refpect will be found a great faving even for the greateft part of the fummer.

The two faddle-horfes were not much in the ftable in the fummer; and the fix acres of each fort, as juft mentioned, befides producing food for my nine draught-horfes, and fome given to cows, fed my faddle-horfes likewife until har-veft, and for a month afterwards: the whole being a period of thirteen months. Some of the wheat-fcouge was left. It is to be noticed, that during the fummer months I had grafs mowed, which was mixed with the cut ftraw.

Now, let the farmer compare this method in point of expence with that which he has been accuftomed to; or let him attend to the calculation of expence of my own for one or two years prior to the time I have been

fpeaking

speaking of. I charge the same number of horses with the rent of a close, for which I

pay	£. 28	7	0
Tythe		1	7	0
Expences of harvesting at 5 s. per acre		2	5	0
	£.31	19	0

If the eddish pays the assessments of different kinds, it is as much as can be expected. I then bought not less than forty pounds worth of hay, exclusive of the expences enumerated. The weekly allowances of corn were two quarters of oats and nine bushels of beans. Next winter when I used chopped straw, I stinted them to a shorter allowance of six bushels of beans, and dropped the use of oats. For six successive weeks I gave them potatoes: but, having found one horse dead in the stable, and in a few days another very ill, I dropped the use of that kind of food: though I am still in doubt whether the potatoes were the cause of his death. As horses are remarkably fond of the root, my man might perhaps give them too great a quantity.

The

The horse which was found dead seemed to have died without pain. He had eaten up all the food given him over night. The men left the stable at nine o'clock in the evening, and, at their return next morning before six, found him lying in such a posture, that they thought him only sleeping: he had not in the least disturbed his litter, which he must have done had he struggled.

I will now state the difference in respect to keep for two winters.

———————

Expences according to the Old Method.

	£.	s.	d.
To hay	71	19	0
2 Quarters of oats weekly— 104 quarters, at 1l. 10s.	156	0	0
9 Bushels of beans weekly— 486 bushels, at 6s.	140	8	0
	£.368	7	0

Expences

Expences according to the Improved Method.

	£.	s.	d.
To six acres of wheat-scouge at 2*l.* 2*s.* per acre	12	12	0
Allowing 1*l.* 1*s.* per acre for the wheat, which is by far more than it is worth, as many farmers would not have accepted of it for thrashing	6	6	0
Six acres of oats, at 10*l.* 10*s.* per acre	63	0	0
Cutting straw; one man, fifty-two weeks, at 12*s.* per week	31	4	0
Six bushels of beans for fifty-two weeks, at 6*s.*	93	12	0

The sum total   £.206 14 0

	£.	s.	d.
First method	368	7	0
Improved ditto	206	14	0

Balance in favour of

the Improved Method   161 13 0

£.368 7 0

The

The work of the horfes was nearly the fame each winter. Twice in every week fix of the nine were ufed to go from Doncaf-ter to Sheffield with a waggon loaded with about 800 gallons of ale. The weight of the waggon and ale exceeded fix tons; con-fequently each horfe had full one ton to draw for his fhare. The diftance between Don-cafter and Sheffield is eighteen miles, which made in the aggregate feventy-two miles per week; but they frequently had to go a mile beyond Sheffield.

The journey to Sheffield and returning home took up moft commonly 22 hours: the fpare days they were employed either going out with ale, or at plough. I could perceive no difference in refpect to the condition of the horfes between the years they were fed according to the firft method, and thofe they were fed, according to the improved method, with ftraw, &c. They performed their work well each year; and they certainly had enough to do.

It may not be unneceffary to obferve, that great part of thofe winters in which the horfes were fed with ftraw, each horfe worked his dray, which weighed about twenty-two hundred

dred weight: but I found this hurt the horfes' backs very much, and therefore gave it up.

In the year 1793, I erected a mill for the purpofe of grinding oats and beans for my horfes. But I was much difappointed: for, contrary to my expectations, I found this to be the worft of all methods; though I perfevered in it for fome time, thinking it might anfwer in the end. At firft I gave the number of horfes before mentioned two quarters of oats and nine bufhels of beans a-week, only a little broken: they foon loft their flefh. I then had both oats and beans ground to meal: but the horfes appeared worfe. Sufpecting that the men poffibly might rob the creatures of their corn, I rofe early and attended them whilft eating their corn, both morning and evening: but, in fpite of all my vigilance, they continued decreafing in flefh. Still I thought it impoffible the corn fhould become worfe by being ground. My men, however, did not like the trouble of grinding: and as at the time we were much hurried with bufinefs, they fometimes neglected it, and at length gave it up entirely; which I was not forry for. I was really afhamed of this fcheme;

for it had coft me upwards of twenty pounds
to erect the mill. I do not here eftimate the
value of the power given to the mill-work,
as that part was made already for the brewery.

I could not in any manner fatisfactorily explain to myfelf why corn fhould be fo much
worfe for grinding; but I faw, a fhort time
after, another proof that it really is fo. I had
occafion to go a journey; and, the weather
being fine, I got upon the box with the ftage-
coachman. He had a pair of very fine leaders
in excellent condition, which I took notice of
and praifed : but the coachman faid, I fhould
fee them fo tired before they got to the end of
the ftage, that he fhould be hardly able to whip
them on. I expreffed my furprife at this, as it
was but a fifteen miles ftage, and afked him
whether his horfes were *foft*. He replied,
No; it was the fault of his mafter, who had
bought a quantity of bran, and mixed it with
ground oats and beans; which food made the
horfes fo weak, that in fuch hot weather as we
then had they could fcarcely crawl after they
had gone three or four miles. " You will
prefently fee them," added the man, " in
fuch a miferably relaxed condition, they will
be

be as white as your fhirt, and fweat in fuch a manner as to make one pity them." The corroborating evidence of the coachman convinced me of the caufe of my horfes looking fo bad: but, being defirous of hearing whether the coachman was capable of giving any reafon for his affertions, I told him, I always underftood that it was beft to feed horfes with ground corn. "Then you underftood wrong, mafter," faid he; "for I know my horfes have been much weaker fince they have been fo fed." "But," faid I, "probably they have lefs now than when they fed upon unground corn." He replied. "No; for they have all they will eat." As this man had fpent his life amongft horfes, in his youth was brought up in the ftable, afterwards a poft-boy, and then a coachman, I had the curiofity to enquire of him how the different mafters he had lived with ufed to keep their horfes. Amongft the number he mentioned, there was one who made ufe of chopped ftraw, with one third of faintfoin and beans, but no oats; and whofe horfes performed their work better and were ftronger than any others he had ever met with. He faid, that for middle-aged horfes the beans were not

fplit;

split; but for the very old, or the very young, they were, and that the harder the beans the better. The quantity of beans given with the faintfoin and ftraw appeared very fcanty to me; but the coachman affured me they were fully fufficient.

I am now convinced that ground corn is not proper to be given to working horfes. If a horfe ftands in the ftable, he will fatten on bran, which will not fupport him if he has common exercife, as his carcafe will foon fhow. A horfe will fatten fooner at grafs in a good pafture, than in a ftable on the beft of corn; but in the latter he acquires a firm hard flefh which will bear work; and in the former only a wafhey foft flefh, which diminifhes with trifling exercife. In fhort, a horfe that ftands in the ftable to be *made up*, will fatten with almoft any thing. I have tried carrots, potatoes, bran-pafte, &c. but the great defideratum is to keep working horfes well and cheap; and, in thirty years' experience, I never yet have found any thing equal to chopped ftraw with corn.

I have tried beans in the ftraw; and excellent food they yield after Candlemas. Peas

are

are improper; for pea-ftraw is fo crooked as to prevent the cutting it fhort enough, and the horfes will throw it out with their nofes.

Great part of the favings arifing from the ufe of wheat-ftraw depends much upon the man who cuts the ftraw, and him who gives it to the horfes. For, if the man who ferves the horfes will not give them a little at a time; but, on the contrary to fave himfelf trouble, throws in one fkuttlefull after another, and continually keeps the manger full, the horfe in that cafe will not thrive, and, inftead of faving, the food recommended will prove ex- penfive. If a fmall quantity at a time were thrown in, the horfe would be enticed to feed; and chopped ftraw, mixed as before directed, would be found to anfwer every purpofe.

Let the horfe continually have a clean man- ger. When he firft comes into the ftable, he will eat the ftraw greedily by itfelf, if you put but a fmall quantity in : when you find he be- gins to tire of ftraw, give him a few beans with it; always taking care to deal out with a very fparing hand, until he is full enough; which is eafily known to an obferving feeder.

In my opinion, if to a quick-feeding hungry
horfe

horfe you were to fpread a quartern of oats with an equal quantity of chopped ftraw, over the bottom of the manger, in fuch a manner that he muft take fome time in licking them up, and be obliged of courfe to chew every oat; it would anfwer the purpofe of twice the quantity of the fame corn thrown into the manger on a heap. For, in the latter inftance he would fwallow the oats whole, and they would pafs through him without being properly digefted. Chopped ftraw is good for making a horfe chew and take pains with his food; and I infift upon it, that he will thrive better on it than on any quantity of corn and hay from natural grafs, given in the ufual manner. Some horfes will eat this kind of food ftill better if it be watered in a tub, before you put it in the manger.

If you take a horfe out of a grafs field in the morning, and give him, according to the cuftom of moft farmers, a feed of corn, and immediately afterwards ride or plough with him, or give him any fatiguing or hard exercife, the corn will be of little ufe, as it will quickly pafs off with his grafs. But, if you with more judgment give him the fame

quantity

quantity of corn over-night, it will then, from the inactivity of the animal, have time to digeſt in his ſtomach.

SECTION XLIV.

Method of Soiling horſes for Husbandry; and the great advantage ariſing therefrom in Summer.

WE have repeatedly taken pains to inculcate the advantage of uſing chopped ſtraw: and in no one inſtance will the farmer find it more highly beneficial than in mixing full half ſtraw cut with the green fodder. It is as bread to meat with human beings; it imbibes the redundant juices of the green food, attenuates the viſcoſity of the humours in the body, promotes the circulation, and the diſcharge of noxious and excrementitious matter, and affords a moſt wholeſome nouriſhment to the horſe, as the ſleekneſs of his coat will bear witneſs.

Soiling a horſe with green food only is very apt to engender corrupt humours in the ſtomach,

mach, and renders the animal too laxative to
support any hard work or violent exercife :
fuch food paffes fuddenly through the horfe ;
and this crudity is moft erroneoufly termed
quick digeftion, not knowing that digeftion
means the diffolution of the food fo minutely
as to enable it to enter the veffels and circulate
with the mafs of blood.

A horfe will eat any fort of grafs, when
mown and laid before him in the ftable or fold.
The bent left in paftures where oxen and
fheep feed, would thus feed a number of
horfes ; as likewife the grafs and weeds under
trees or hedges. Some tether a horfe in thofe
places : this is better than not eating the grafs
at all. But nothing is fo good as mowing ; as
by that means the horfe makes manure, and
the grafs grows finer. On the contrary the
part on which the horfe is tethered, gets coarfer
and coarfer ; for he depofits all his urine and
dung upon the very fpot of ground where he
ought not. Road-fides, and all places where
weeds and fmall quantity of grafs grow, are
worth mowing, were it only for making manure.—Indeed, weeds in highways ought always

ways to be cut down, to prevent the feeds fhaking; for thiftle-feed will blow for miles. There are in fome fields near London more thiftles than corn, from neglecting, I fuppofe, to deftroy them before the feed ripens. If the above cautions were attended to, there would be no want of manure in places where the produce of the land is confumed upon the farm.

There are many other advantages attending the foiling horfes in the ftable: but as they have been frequently fpoken of in this work, it is needlefs to fay more here.

SECTION XLV.

Observations made by the Author in valuing Es-
tates for different Gentlemen, describing the Old
and New System of Husbandry: with Debtor
and Creditor Account: the great Advantage of
the New System, in many instances from 50 to
100 per cent.

MY first observation is upon a tillage farm
in the neighbourhood of Doncaster, consisting
of 139 acres. I shall first describe the management, and next the method which ought to
be pursued. To make each as clear as possible,
I lay down the following debtor and creditor
account, beginning with the Old System.

Rotation of Crops used under the Old System.

Dr. to EXPENCES.	£.	s.	d.	Cr. by PRODUCE.	£.	s.	d.
To 23 acres wheat, ploughing, sowing, &c. at 7s. per acre - - -	8	1	0	Wheat, 23 acres, at 7 loads per acre, at 18s. per load - - -	144	18	0
Seed, 23 loads, at 18s. per load -	20	14	0	Barley, 9 ditto, at 4 qrs. per acre at 25s. per quarter	45	0	0
Reaping, leading, &c. at 10s. per acre - - -	11	10	0	Oats, 23 ditto, at 4 qrs. per acre at 12s. per quarter	55	4	0
	40	5	0		245	2	0

Dr. *to* EXPENCES.	£.	s.	d.
Brought over	40	5	0
Thrashing, dref- fing, 161 loads, at 1s. per load -	8	1	0
Mowing ftubble 3s. per acre - -	3	9	0
9 acres of barley, ploughing, &c. at 7s. per acre -	3	3	0
Seed, 4 quar. 4 bufh. at 25s. per quar.	5	12	6
Reaping, leading, &c. at 8s. per acre - -	3	12	0
Thrashing, &c. 36 qrs. at 1s. 6d. per qr. - - -	2	14	0
23 acres oats, ploughing, &c. at 7s. per acre .	8	1	0
Seed, 14 qrs. 3 bufh. at 12s. per qr. -	8	12	6
Reaping, leading, &c. at 6. per acre	6	18	0
Thrashing, &c. 92 qrs. at 1s. per qr.	4	12	0
4½ acres of beans, ploughing, &c. at 7s. per acre -	1	11	6
Seed, 2 qrs. 2 bufh- els, at 24s. per quar. - - - -	2	14	0
Reaping, &c. at 8s. per acre - -	1	16	0
12 acres hay, har- vefting, at 5s. per acre - - -	3	0	0
	£ 104	1	6

Cr. *by* PRODUCE.	£	s.	d.
Brought over	245	2	0
Beans 4½ ditto, at 3 ditto per acre, at 24s. per qr. -	16	4	0
59½ ac. under plough			
20 in fallow			
59½ in grafs			
139 total quant. of acres,			
59½ acres ftraw, &c. at 1*l.* per acre -	59	10	0
12 ditto hay, at 1 ton per acre, 4*l.* per ton - -	48	0	0
Profit on 5 cows, at 5*l.* 5*s.* per cow	26	5	0
Profit a bull makes per annum -	5	5	0
9 wethers - -	18	0	0
20 fat lambs - -	15	0	0
Wool, 30 fleeces, at 3s. each -	4	10	0
1 horfe (fuppofe) fold in 2 years, will be the half of a horfe in this year's profits -	8	0	0
Pigs - - - -	5	0	0
	£ 450	16	0

	L.	s.	d.
Brought over	104	1	6
20 acres fallow, four times ploughing, &c. at 5s. 6d. per acre - -	22	0	0
142 loads of manure at 8s. per load -	56	16	0
Rent - - -	110	0	0
Assessments, at 5s	27	10	0
	320	7	6
	130	8	6
	450	16	0

	L.	s.	d.
Brought over,	450	16	0
Errors excepted. £450	16	0

Rotation of Crops under the New System.

Dr. to EXPENCES. | **Cr. by PRODUCE.**

Dr. to EXPENCES.	L.	s.	d.
20 Acres in Turnip Fallow.			
2 ploughings, &c. carrying twitch off, &c. at 7s. each	14	0	0
6 loads manure per acre, leading on, &c. 8s. per load	48	0	0
Drilling at 2s. 6d. per acre - -	2	10	0
Seed, 6d. per acre	0	10	0
Hoeing, and 3 times ploughing, 2s. each time per acre -	6	0	0
20 Acres Wheat Crop.			
Ploughing, sowing, &c. 7s. per acre -	7	0	0
Seed, 20 loads, 18s. per load - -	18	0	0
£96	0	0

Cr. by PRODUCE.	L.	s.	d.
20 acres turnips, at 4l. per acre	80	0	0
20 ditto wheat, 8 loads per acre 18s. per load	144	0	0
20 ditto peas, at 12 loads per do. 12s. per load	144	0	0
20 ditto barley, at 4 qrs. per ditto, 25s. per qr. -	100	0	0
20 ditto clover, at 2 ton per ditto, 4l. per ton -	160	0	0
20 ditto wheat, at 8 loads per ditto, 18s. per load -	144	0	0
80 acres straw, 20s. per acre -	80	0	0
£852	0	0

	£.	s.	d.
Brought over,	96	0	0
Reaping and leading, 10s. per acre - - - -	10	0	0
160 loads thrashing, &c. 1s. per load - - -	8	0	0
Stubble mowing, &c. 3s. per acre,	3	0	0

20 *Acres Peas Crop.*

	£.	s.	d.
Ploughing, harrowing, &c. twice, 7s. per acre each -	14	0	0
Seed 10 quarters, at 32s. per quarter	16	0	0
Drill. 2s. 6d. per acre - - -	2	10	0
4 loads manure per acre, leading, &c. at 8s per load -	32	0	0
3 ploughings per ac. 1s. 6d. per ac. each	4	10	0
Reaping and thrashing 240 loads, at 8d. per load	8	0	0

20 *Acres Barley Crop.*

	£.	s.	d.
Ploughing, &c. and sowing, 7s. per ac.	7	0	0
Seed, 4 bush. per ac. at 25s. per qr.	12	10	0
Clover-feed, 14lb. trefoil, 6lb.	8	10	0
Reaping and leading, at 8s. per ac.	8	0	0
Thrashing, &c. 30 qrs. 1s. 6d. per qr.	6	0	0
	£ 236	0	0

	£.	s.	d.
Brought over.	852	0	0
Profit brought from account of 10 acres managed according to New System See p. 216 -	80	0	0
	£ 932	0	0

	£.	s.	d.
Brought over - 236	0	0
20 *Acres Clover-Grafs.*		
6 loads manure per ac. 8s. per load	48	0	0
Mowing, &c. twice, 6s. per acre	12	0	0
20 *Acres Wheat Crop.*		
Ploughing, fowing, &c. 7s. per acre	7	0	0
Seed, 20 loads, 18s. per load	18	0	0
Reaping and leading, 10s. per ac.	10	0	0
Thrashing, &c. at 1s. per load	8	0	0
Stubble mowing 3s. per acre	3	0	0
Rent and affeff-ments	137	10	0
	479	10	0
Profit - -	452	10	0
	£ 932	0	0

	£.	s.	d.
Brought over - 932	0	0
	£932	0	0

Errors excepted.

We will fuppofe the farm-houfes, barns, and buildings in general, together with the fences on the whole farm, to occupy by ad-meafurement nine acres of land. There will then remain ten acres for fupport of the cows, horfes, &c. The beft method to make the ten acres anfwer that purpofe will be to fow three and a half of them with winter tares;

two

two and a half with fummer cabbages, and
potatoes under them ; and the remaining four
with fpring tares : or you may fow part of
them with buck-wheat. I mean thofe ten
acres to fupply the place of the 59½ acres allowed for the fame ufe in the Old Syftem, always fuppofing in both cafes that the buildings, fences, &c. take up nine acres.

Thefe ten acres will moft certainly coft
fomething tilling and managing : but, if carefully looked after, they will maintain forty
head of cattle and horfes in fummer, with the
affiftance of chopped ftraw, as before defcribed:
and the farmer will have one hundred and
twenty acres of ftraw, clover, &c. where he
had before in the old method only fifty-nine
and a half ; and he may be certain that every
crop by this management will be more bulky,
and his quantity of manure continually increafe by keeping forty head of cattle and
horfes in the fold, winter and fummer, not to
mention pigs. As the food I have recommended is too rich for breeding ftock, if the
farmer keeps fix cows, as before mentioned,
he will want twenty-fix feeding beafts, which
may average at five guineas each; but much
more

more may be made—he may make two re-turns. However, as the profits accruing by this method may appear incredible to thofe who fet their faces againft any innovation or improvement, I will explain myfelf by a debtor and creditor account.

We will fuppofe the ten acres to be at firft fet with potatoes to make the land ready and clean for the tares, &c. Carry the profit on the potatoes to the general account, as it is part of the crop for the firft year of the New Method.

New Syftem on Ten Acres of Potatoes.

Dr. to EXPENCES.	£.	s.	d.	Cr. by PRODUCE.	£.	s.	d.
Ploughing 10 acres at 7s. per acre	3	10	0	By 10 acres, fold at 10l. 10s. per acre	105	0	0
120 facks of potatoes for feed, at 3s. per fack	18	0	0				
Harrowing at different times, 2s. per acre - - -	1	0	0				
Ploughing up, at 5s per acre - -	2	10	0				
Profit carried to the Gen. Account of one year's profit	80	0	0				
	£105	0	0		£105	0	0

N. B. The potatoe crop is suppofed to be fold on the land, as it is difficult to calculate expences when they are fold by the farmer at market, or he would make more than double the fum mentioned; for one hundred facks, at 3s. per fack, would be 15l. per acre, which would be 150l. : but, if well fet and managed, he would have an hundred and fifty facks per acre.

Ten Acres of Land, &c. managed by the New Syftem.

Dr. to EXPENCES.	£.	s.	d	Cr. by PRODUCE.	£.	s.	d.
3½ acres ploughing harrowing and fowing, at 7s. per acre	1	4	6	By the profit on 32 beafts, at an average of 5l. 5s. per beaft	168	0	0
Seed tares, 2 bufhels per ac. at 10s. per bufhel, and ½ peck of rye at 6d pr. peck	3	11	9				
1½ acre of cabbages ploughing, &c. 7s. per acre	0	10	6				
2½ acres drilling, at 2s. 6d. per acre	0	6	3				
	£5	13	0		£168	0	0

	£.	s.	d.		£.	s.	d.
Brought over -	5	13	c	Brought over -	168	0	0
Plants which muft be raifed on a feed-bed. 4lb. of feed, at 6s. per lb. digging the garden and fow- ing	1	9	c				
Planting, at 5s. per acre	0	12	6				
4 acres, 3 times ploughing and fowing, at 7s, per acre	4	4	c				
Manure for 10 ac. every year, at 4 loads per acre, at 8s. per load	16	0	0				
Profit by this mode	140	1	6				
	168	0	c		168	0	0

The above balance of profit certainly appears great: but the uncommon quantity of food the ten acres will fupply by the tares and rye raifed upon them (when chopped with wheat ftraw as before defcribed) is really incredible to thofe who have not given this method a fair trial. I have kept ten horfes thirteen months on fix acres of wheat-fcouge, and fix acres of oats. From this it may eafily be conceived, that ten acres of green fodder, with

with ten acres of wheat-ftraw, will keep forty
head of cattle and horfes during the fummer.
Forty acres of wheat-ftraw, twenty acres of
clover twice mown, twenty acres of barley-
ftraw, and twenty acres of pea ftraw, together
with twenty acres of turnips, will eafily keep
thirty-two head of beafts and eight horfes
during the winter. No one can fuppofe that
I mean the ten acres alone fhould keep the
number of the different cattle mentioned. I
mean, that the produce of the ten acres ap-
propriated to the raifing of green fodder,
if you mix it with the ftraw and clover in
manner as directed, and properly and regularly
feed the cattle, will be found to anfwer the
purpofe, and render every fervice I have afferted it capable of performing.

Cabbages of the early kind will be ready to
cut the beginning of June; and you may
keep cutting all fummer, as, before you have
got through a certain quantity, the fprouts of
fome will be ready to cut again. It is meant
that thefe cabbages fhould be given to fuch
beafts as are in the beft condition, or neareft
ready for market. When you have cut your
winter

winter tares and rye, favoy cabbages muft be put in the land. You will mow your tares in fummer; and the cabbages will ferve the cattle in winter, and be foon enough removed from the ground to fow it with tares in the fpring. Where the fpring cabbages grow, you muft in autumn fow winter tares in drills. Put in four or fix loads of manure per acre to every crop. Thefe ten acres are, like a garden, continually to be covered with crops; I efteem them as much a garden for the ufe of the cattle, as I do the kitchen-garden for the ufe of the family.

Although I have calculated twenty acres of turnips to be ufed for the feeding of cattle in the fold; they will not all be wanted, but one half, or perhaps more, may be eaten with fheep. Therefore a profit will arife, of which no notice has here been taken. The quantity of manure calculated in the New Syftem is very much lefs than will arife; but as the method is fo new in this and in moft other parts, I very much wifh to avoid placing over much profit before the reader at once. Honey is a fweet thing; but if I had never feen any, and

by

by any chance had met with fome in the trunk of a tree, I fhould be afraid to tafte it: but if I at laft fhould venture and get one lick, I fhould be inclined to tafte again ; and when I found it both fweet to my tafte, and whole-fome, I fhould become fond of it. So much do I expect this New Syftem of farming will prove pleafant to the farmer, when he once taftes the fweets of it. There is nothing fweetens labour fo much as an adequate re-ward ; and method is the foul of all bufinefs. By the rules laid down in this Treatife a farm becomes almoft as productive as a garden ; and I would ftimulate every one to exert him-felf to follow them in practice. I have been ufed to feed cattle upon the moft fertile grounds in the county of Lincoln, but never could arrive at fuch a ftate of perfection as by this method. It may not be amifs to obferve, that in two different inftances I have fo well fattened two Scotch cows, that they had as much tallow within them, as they weighed per quarter, though they had been milked within fix weeks of their being killed, the one weigh-ed four ftone per quarter, and had four ftone

of

of fat in her : the other nine ftone per quarter, and had nine ftone of fat in her.

Now fuppofe to the New Method we allow one man and one boy extra to look after the cattle, horfes, &c. We will eftimate the man at 12*s.* per week, and the boy at 6*s.* per week. Though thefe wages may appear at firft fight rather extravagant, yet, as Sunday's attendance will be required for a part of the day at leaft, we will be liberal in our pay: therefore, throwing away the odd day, the hours and minutes, and reckoning fifty-two weeks for the year, we have the fum of 46*l.* 16*s.* to deduct, which will leave a balance of 405*l.* 14*s.* Now the profit by the Old Syftem is 130*l.* 3*s.* 6*d.* which taken from 405*l.* 14*s*, leaves a net difference in profit in favour of the New Syftem of 275*l.* 5*s.* 6*d.*

In the Old Syftem we reckoned the profit of a horfe in two years fixteen pounds, the half of which, taking only one year's, will be 8*l.* and of pigs, as before, 5*l.* Thefe fums added to 275*l.* 5*s.* 6*d.* will make in the aggregate 288*l.* 5*s.* 6*d.*

The 80*l.* for the potatoes only have been
brought

brought to account : but the net profit from
the ten acres in green crops, being 140*l*. 1*s*. 6*d*.
will make the aggregate fum 348*l*. 7*s*. 0*d*.
which appears a very large fum : but by this
method of cultivation and feeding of cattle,
it will be found that manure will be made of fo
much better quality, and in fuch plenty, and
at fo much cheaper rate than by buying, which
has been the general practice in this neighbourhood, that a farmer who lives four or fix miles
from a poft or manufacturing town, will fcarcely be at the trouble of fetching it ; and manure, being the mafter-piece of all agriculture,
will raife every crop to be fo abundant as to
give aftonifhment to the beholders of them.

There are feveral advantages in refpect to
fituation attending this farm in the vicinity
of Doncafter, which from their locality will
not apply to the other two farms I mean to
treat of. I have from experience learned that
garden-peas of the early fort, fet in the month
of January as here before defcribed, will be
more productive than any field-peas, and always fell at a better price, even if you harveft
them. But you have a chance of felling a

part

part in the pods green, which may fetch twenty guineas per acre at the leaft, and you may have a crop of turnips after with eafe : but this crop of turnips has not been taken into the account. It may be faid the profit on the beafts is laid too high; but I deny that to be the cafe, for the following reafons. When you feed cattle on grafs, it is poffible that the feafons may vary fo much that the fame pafture might keep double the number of cattle at one time to what it may be capable of at another. Therefore as it is ufual to put in the fame number every year, fhould the feafon prove dry, you probably will be overloaded with ftock : if, on the contrary, it fhould prove wet, you will be deficient in flock; and in either of thefe cafes you will be difappointed. But with food provided in the manner defcribed above, your green crops get fo forward before the dry feafon probably arrives, that they receive no injury; and by fold or ftable-feeding the animal, if chofen of the right fort, to a certainty fpeedily becomes fat. His food, his work, his reft is regular, every day is the fame; and every day will he

increafe

increase, to the emolument of his owner. And as Rotherham market is within six miles, the farmer has an opportunity to sell his own beasts; and if the price offered for them proves not to his satisfaction, he can drive them home, and take them another day to market. A sort of jobbing business may be carried on by attending such a market, to sell in dear markets, and buy in cheap ones; and likewise the business of selling cows and calves, by buying in cows with calf, and keeping them to calve, to make fat the calves, and milk the cows a sufficient time, and then fatten them. A crop of early potatoes may be raised on some part of the land intended for turnips, and sold in time to have a crop of turnips after; and should he be short of his green crop, he has a crop of clover continually on the land, in summer, which secures him food for his cattle on a certainty. His farm is within the compass, that an industrious man may see that every part of his business is executed properly; and he does not require so strong a team to carry his corn to market; nor need his servant be so long absent from his home employ; and he can scarcely go to any market with his corn but he may bring coals back.

It is to be obferved that in the foregoing calculations I have fuppofed all the ploughing, and fowing, and leading, fhould be hired and paid for. Thefe accounts, as drawn out, lean much in favour of the Old Syftem, as the expences are fewer in number than will really be found in following that method. The calculations are made for the purpofe of fhewing at one view the great difparity which will actually be found to exift in the practice of the two different methods, on fimilar farms. As to afcertaining the profits exactly, that is impoffible; as the markets fluctuate in fo great a degree, that no one can be correct in the valuation of cattle or corn for fix months forward. I have conftantly eftimated the expences at a high.r rate than I know they may be done at, that I might not be fuppofed to deal unfairly with the Old Method.

The fecond farm I mean to treat of is, of the grazing, breeding, and ploughing kind. It is fituated in Lincolnfhire, and confifts of three hundred and fourteen acres. Part of it

is

is at prefent divided into four plats for ploughing, each plat confifting of twenty-four acres.
There is an additional plat of the fame kind
of land, containing fixteen acres ;* and about
fourteen acres of clay-land, which is alfo
ploughed. Thefe, added together, make one
hundred and twenty-fix acres, all under plough
according to the old management. If you
fubtract the one hundred and twenty-fix acres
from three hundred and fourteen, there will
be a refidue of one hundred and eighty-eight
acres, which are all in grafs, and ufed for the
purpofe of raifing one hundred and forty lambs,
or tupping one hundred and forty ewes (as the
hogs are fold off in fpring, and the drape ewes
at Michaelmas,) and keeping twelve horfes,
and thirty beafts. The rotation of crops here
made ufe of is according to the old fyftem, as
before obferved, viz. turnips, barley, clover
and wheat: and probably the method here
followed may be as good as any other ; as the

farm

---

* The four plats confifting of twenty-four acres each,
and the plat of fixteen acres, are of limeftone: the reft
clay, and liable to rot fheep.

farm is applied to the breeding of sheep, the most lucrative business the farmer can pursue. I will now state a debtor and creditor account of the expences and produce of the farm, as now managed.

The present Rotation of Crops in a Year,

Dr. to EXPENCES.	Cr. by PRODUCE.

FIRST PLAT.

	£. s. d		£. s. d.
To fallowing 24 acres for turnips; 4 times ploughing, harrowing, &c. at 6s. per acre each	28 16 0	By 24 acres turnips, at 3l. 10s. per acre	84 0 0
12 Loads manure per acre, at 8s.	115 4 0	24 Acres barley, 4 quarters per acre, at 25s per quarter	110 0 0
Seed and hoeing, 6s. per acre	7 4 0	24 Acres clover, 1½ ton per acre, 1l. per ton	36 0 0
SECOND.		24 Acres clover eaten off, at 10s. 6d. per acre	12 12 0
Ploughing 24 acres for barley, 7s. per acre	8 8 0	24 Acres wheat, 3 quarters per acre at 2l. per quarter	144 0 0
Seed, four bushels per acre, at 25s. per quarter	15 0 0	16 Acres of cliffland, which appear to be carried on in the same manner, but do not seem to be regular in any crop. Therefore	
Clover-seed, 14 lb. per acre, 6d. per lb.	8 8 0		
Reaping and leading 6s. per acre	7 4 0		
Trashing, &c. 96 quarters, at 1s. 4d. per quarter	6 8 0		
	£.196 12 0		£.396 12 0

Dr. to EXPENCE.	£. s. d.	Cr. by PRODUCE.	£. s. d.
Brt. over.	196 12 0	Brt. over.	396 12 0
THIRD.		I will take the	
Clover, mowing		average of its	
&c. 24 acres, 3s.		produce from the	
per acre	3 12 0	produce of the	
FOURTH.		96 acres above,	
24 Acres ploughing		which are regu-	
for wheat, 7s per		larly cropped	
acre	8 8 0	(as the land is	
Seed, 3 bushels per		of the same	
acre, at 5s. per		kind); but be-	
bushel	18 0 0	ing rather bet-	
Reaping and lead-		ter, will say 4l.	
ing, 10s. per acre	12 0 0	10s. per acre	72 0 0
Thrashing, &c. 72		7 Acres of wheat	
quarters, 1s. 8d.		on clay land, at	
per quarter	6 0 0	3 quarters per	
Stubble mowing,		acre, at 2l. per	
3s. per acre	3 12 0	quarter	42 0 0
Average expence		7 Acres beans on	
upon the 16 acres		ditto, 3 quarters	
of cliff land	43 1 0	per acre, 1l. 4s.	
Fallowing ¼ of 14		per quarter	25 4 0
acres of clay land	6 10 8	65 Hogs (feeders)	
Manure once in 3		at 1l. 8s. each	91 0 0
years	16 16 0	50 Ewes (drape)	
Rent and assess-		at 1l. 8s. each	70 0 0
ments	316 4 4½	200 Fleeces of	
Profit	318 9 11½	wool, 1l. 1s. per	
		tod, 4 fleeces	
		to a tod	52 10 0
		6 Fat beasts, 25l.	
		each	150 0 0
		2 Horses, at 20l.	
		each	40 0 0
		Pigs	10 0 0
	£.949 6 0		£.949 6 0
		Profit brt. down	318 9 11½

The New System on the Four Plats of Twenty-four Acres each, and Sixteen Acres,

Dr. to EXPENCES.	Cr. by PRODUCE.

	£. s. d.		£. s. d.
FIRST PLAT.		By 24 acres of turnips, 3l. 10s. per acre	84 0 0
To ploughing &c. twice for turnips on 24 acres twitch &c. raking off, at 6s. per acre	14 8 0	24 Acres barley, 4 quarters per acre, 1l. 5s. per quarter	120 0 0
Drilling and sowing, 2s. 6d. per acre	3 0 0	Clover eat by sheep carried to General Account	
Seed 1s. per acre	1 4 0	24 Acres wheat, 3 quarters per acre, 2l. per quarter	144 0 0
Hoeing and 3 times ploughing, 1s. 6d. per acre	5 8 0	16 Acres saintfoin, 2 ton per acre,	
6 Loads manure per ac. 8s. per load	57 12 0	2l. per ton	64 0 0
SECOND.			
Ploughing &c. and sowing 24 acres for barley, 7s. per acre	8 8 0		
Seed, four bushels, at 25s. per quarter	15 0 0		
Red clover 14 lb. per acre, at 6d. per lb : trefoil 6 lb. per acre, at 3d. per lb : white clover 6 lb. per acre, at 8d. per lb.	15 0 0		
Reaping and leading, 6s. per acre	7 4 0		
£.127 4 0		**£.412 0 0**	

Cr. to EXPENCES.	£.	s.	d.	Cr. by PRODUCE.	£.	s.	d.
Brt. over	127	4	0	Brt. over	412	0	0
Thrashing 96 quarters, at 2s. 4d. per quarter	6	8	0				
THIRD.							
To clover 24 acres eaten by sheep							
FOURTH.							
24 Acres wheat, ploughing &c. 7s. per acre	8	8	0				
Seed, 3 bushels per acre, at 5s. per bushel	18	0	0				
Reaping &c. 10s. per acre	12	0	0				
72 Quarters wheat thrashing, &c. 1s. 8d. per quarter	9	0	0				
Stubble mowing, 3s. per acre	2	12	0				
FIFTH.							
16 Acres saintfoin mowing, 3s. per acre	2	8	0				
Profit	228	0	0				
	£.412	0	0		£.412	0	0
				Profit brt. down £.228		0	0

The General Account of Expence and Produce on the New System on the Lincolnshire Farm, of Eighty-four Acres, which at present rots Sheep.

Dr. to EXPENCES.	£. s. d.	Cr. by PRODUCE.	£. s. d.
FIRST.			
14 Acres wheat, ploughing, &c. 7s. per acre	4 18 0	By 14 acres of wheat, 3½ quarters per acre, at 2 l. per quarter	98 0 0
Seed 3 bushels per acre, 5s. per bushel	10 10 0	14 Acres peas or beans, 4 quarters per acre, 1l. 4s. per quarter	67 4 0
Reaping, &c. 10s. per acre	7 0 0	14 Acres barley, 4 quarters per acre, at 1l. 5s. per qr.	70 0 0
Thrashing, &c. 49 quarters, 1s. 8d. per quarter	4 1 8	14 Acres clover, 2½ tons per acre, at 2l. per ton	70 0 0
Stubble mowing, 3s. per acre	2 2 0	14 Acres wheat, 4 quarters per acre, 2l. per quarter	112 0 0
SECOND.		14 Acres beans, 4 quarters per acre, 1l. 4s. per quarter	67 4 0
14 Acres beans or peas ploughing, &c. 7s. per acre	4 18 0	Profit brought from the 4 plats	228 0 0
Drilling, 2s. 6d. per acre	1 15 0	Profit on beasts, horses, sheep, wool, pigs &c. brought from Account in Old System, being the same in New	413 10 0
4 Loads manure per acre, 8s. per load	22 8 0		
3 Times ploughing, 1s. 4d. each per acre	2 16 0		
Reaping &c. 6s. per acre	4 4 0		
Thrashing &c. 56 quarters, 1s. per quarter	2 16 0		
	£.67 8 8		£.1125 18 0

Dr. to EXPENCES.				Cr. by PRODUCE.		
	£.	s.	d.		£.	s.	d.
Brt. over	67	8	8	Brt. over	1125	18	0
THIRD.							
14 Acres barley, ploughing, 7s. per acre	4	18	0				
Seed, 4 bufhels per acre, 1l. 5s. per quarter	8	15	0				
Clover-feed, 14 lb. per acre, at 6d. per lb. : 6 lb. tre-foil, 3d. per lb.	5	19	0				
Reaping and lead-ing, 8s. per acre	5	12	0				
Thrafhing 56 quar-ters. 1s. 2d. per quarter	3	5	4				
FOURTH.							
14 Acres clover, mowing, &c. 6s. per acre	4	4	0				
6 Loads manure per acre, 8s. per load	33	12	0				
FIFTH.							
14 Acres wheat, ploughing, &c. 7s. per acre	4	18	0				
Seed, 3 bufhels per acre, 5s. per bufhel	10	10	0				
Reaping, &c. 10s. per acre	7	0	0				
Thrafhing, &c. 56 quarters, 1s. 8d. per quarter	4	13	4				
Stubble mowing, 3s. per acre	2	2	0				
	£.162	17	4		£.1125	18	0

Dr. to EXPENCES.		£.	s.	d.	Cr. by PRODUCE.	£.	s.	d.
Brt. over		162	17	4	Brt. over	1125	18	0
SIXTH.								
14 Acres beans, ploughing, &c. 7s. per acre		4	18	0				
Drilling 2s. 6d. per acre		1	15	0				
6 loads manure per acre, 8s. per ld.		33	12	0				
3 times plough-ing 1s. 6d. each per acre		3	3	0				
Reaping, thrashing, &c.		7	0	0				
Rent and affeffment as in the Old Syf-tem Account	316	4	4½					
Profit	596	8	3½					
		£.1125	18	0		£1125	18	0

ERRORS EXCEPTED.

Having thus ftated the management of the Lincolnfhire farm according to the New Me-thod ; it is now neceffary to give fuch an elu-cidation as that the reader may perfectly un-derftand it. What I propofe is the following.

100 Acres of grafs, 3 fheep to every
    two acres   150 *fheep*

10 ditto for feeding beafts, and a
    few tups   4 *tups*

72 ditto for ploughing (in 3 plats)
    as before defcribed. Including

24 ditto fown with graffes to keep
    fheep upon, five to an acre 120 *fheep*
                        —————
                        274

84 ditto clay foil under rotation of crops.
16 ditto of faintfoin for hay.
 8 ditto of meadow to cut green, for the pur-
———— pofe of foiling horfes in the fold or
314 *acres.* ftable:

Which, as we have fhown, is the moft beneficial method of keeping them, and beyond
comparifon preferable to letting them o-
ver the grafs, if only for the benefit of the
manure, which will be found of fuch infinite
value to the farm.

    I fhould keep on this farm at leaft forty
head of beafts and horfes in the ftable and fold,
winter and fummer; but on fuch a farm as
                            this

this twice that number might be kept, and the manure made in fummer with green food by this method would be found to be much better than the manure made in winter in the ufual way. Mixing ftraw intimately in fummer with grafs, clover, or any other green food, as before defcribed, will certainly be applying the ftraw to a much more profitable purpofe than the prefent method of ufing it will admit of; and the cattle, inftead of being poor and pining, would be kept in a thriving ftate, and the manure be bettter in quality in proportion to their good condition. In winter an equal quantity of nutritious food fhould be mixed with the ftraw, fuch as faintfoin or clover hay, potatoes or cabbages, which will preferve the animals in a healthy ftate, and caufe them to increafe in bulk and value.

It does not abfolutely follow that the farmer's cattle muft be poor and pining, becaufe he has not immediately on his farm clover, tares, potatoes or cabbages, carrots, &c.; though alike neceffary and pleafant, as well for his own ufe as that of his cattle. If, at his firft entrance on a farm, he fhould find it deftitute of thefe

neceffary

neceffary articles; by attention and a little art
they may all be foon raifed at a fmall expence:
and ftall-feeding would be attended with much
lefs expence than is generally apprehended, if
a little care were taken in the management;
for I am firmly of opinion that one man and
a boy are fufficient to look after forty head of
cattle, to cut the ftraw and mix it with their
green food in fummer, and with their hay in
winter. But, fuppofing the cattle double that
number, a machine worked by a horfe might
be erected in fome proper place, which might
perform various operations, fuch as thrafhing
of corn, cutting of ftraw, &c. Such a machine
would at firft coft money; and the farmer muft
have a capital to fpare to enable him to erect
it: but he will ftill have but *one* rent to pay for
his farm, the produce will be doubled; his
bufinefs will be near him, and his ftock in a
thriving ftate; he feels himfelf comfortable,
and is the admiration of his neighbours.

The difagreeable circumftance of the land
rotting fheep, the reader will obferve, is done
away by ploughing the eighty-four acres of
clay-land, and eating the feeds, faintfoin, eddish

difh, &c. By ftall-feeding the greateft part of
horfes will be kept up; for nothing is fo hurt-
ful in rotting of fheep on land, as horfes going
upon it, or in fact any other land, except perhaps when you turn a fmall number of them
into a clofe; as horfes will eat fome kinds of
grafs which no other animals will touch : fuch,
for example, as grows againft fences and by
the fides of footpaths. It will neverthelefs be
found a much better and cheaper method to
keep them in folds, as before directed, than in
paftures, where they do more harm with their
feet than with their mouths.

The number of fheep will be increafed feventy. Therefore, if my calculation is right,
inftead of felling the hogs, they may be kept
for wethers. Should any danger be apprehended of the rot, add to the number of beafts
(which perhaps may turn out as profitable by
having a greater quantity in the fold), and
keep only the old number of fheep, viz. two
hundred to clip : and the feeds in the fpring
fhould be eaten up by four fheep to an acre.
I mean thofe twenty-four acres, part of the
ninety-fix in the foregoing eftimate, and which

we

we calculated to maintain five sheep by being
sown with seeds: but we will put the even
number of one hundred upon these twenty-four
acres; fifty of the best sheeder hogs; and fifty
of the best shearling ewes: only one hundred
sheep then remain, for one hundred acres of
grafs-land: of courfe, there would be an opportunity of keeping many beafts, or of mea-
dowing fome of the land.

It is the general cuftom to fell off the drape
ewes. Now, by taking the lambs from them
very early in the month of June, or in July at
fartheft, the ewes would have fufficient time to
get fat before winter, and then be fold as fat
ewes; and the fixteen acres of faintfoin eddifh
would infure a net profit on the fheep fuperior
to what is generally made. The lambs might
be taken to the faintfoin, which would preferve
them found while the ewes are getting fat.

The third farm alluded to.

We fhall now give a Dr. and Cr. Statement
of a Rotation of Crops for fix years on the Old
System

Syftem, ufed in a great many parts of Yorkfhire as the beft. This is taken from an acre
of land from an extenfive eftate in the North
Riding, confifting of feveral hundred acres of
open tillage land.

Courfe of Hufbandry—One fallow and two
crops, viz. 1ft year fallow, manured—2nd year,
barley—3d year, beans—4th year, fallow—5th
year, wheat—6th year, oats.

*Rotation of Crops for Six Years on the Old
Syftem.*

Dr. to EXPENCES.	Cr. by PRODUCE.
1ft YEAR FALLOW.	
£. s. d.	
To 4 ploughings and harrowings, &c. at 7s. 1 8 0	By no crop
12 Loads of manure, at 8s. per load 4 16 0	
One year's rent 0 15 0	
Affeffments 0 10 0	
Tythe 0 6 0	
£7 15 0	

Dr. to EXPENCES.	£. s. d.	Cr. by PRODUCE	£. s. d.

2d YEAR, BARLEY.

Dr. to EXPENCES.	£. s. d.	Cr. by PRODUCE	£. s. d.
To ploughing and harrowing	0 6 6	By 4 quarters of barley, at 1l. 5s.	5 0 0
Seed, 4 bushels	0 12 6	Straw	1 0 0
Reaping & thrashing	0 12 6		
Rent	0 15 0		
Assessment	0 10 0		
Tythe	0 6 0		
	£3 2 6		£6 0 0

3d YEAR, BEANS.

Dr. to EXPENCES.	£. s. d.	Cr. by PRODUCE	£. s. d.
To ploughing and harrowing	0 6 6	By 3 quarters of beans, at 1l. 12s. per quarter	4 16 0
Seed, 4 bushels	0 16 0	Straw	1 0 0
Reaping & thrashing	0 12 0		
Rent	0 15 0		
Assessments	0 10 0		
Tythe	0 6 0		
	£3 5 6		£5 16 0

4th YEAR FALLOW.

Dr. to EXPENCES.	£. s. d.	Cr. by PRODUCE
To ploughing, three times harrowing, &c.	1 1 0	By no crop
Rent	0 15 0	
Assessments	0 10 0	
Tythe	0 6 0	
	£2 12 0	

Dr. to EXPENCES.	£.	s.	d.	Cr. by PRODUCE.	£.	s.	d.
5th YEAR WHEAT.							
To ploughing	0	5	0	By 3 quarters of wheat, at 2l. 10s.			
Seed-wheat, three bushels	0	18	9	per quarter	7	10	0
Rent	0	15	0	Straw	1	0	0
Assessments	0	10	0				
Tythe	0	6	0				
Reaping & thrash-ing	0	15	0				
	£3	9	9		£8	10	0
6th YEAR OATS.							
To ploughing and harrowing	0	6	6	By 4 quarters of oats, at 16s. per			
Seed, 4 bushels	0	8	0	quarter	3	4	0
Rent	0	15	0	Straw	1	0	0
Assessments	0	10	0				
Tythe	0	6	0				
Reaping and lead-ing	0	6	6				
Thrashing	0	4	0				
	£2	16	0		£4	4	0
				Total of the Cr. side	£24	10	0
				Total of the Dr. ditto	23	0	9
				Profit on one acre of land for six years	£. 1	9	3

A Rotation of Crops for fix years, upon the
fame land as above, by the New Syftem, as follows :—1ft year, turnip fallow—2nd year, barley—3d year, peas fallow—4th year, wheat or
oats—5th year, clover—6th year, wheat.

Rotation of Crops for fix Years by the New
Syftem.

Dr. *to* EXPENCES.				Cr. *by* PRODUCE.			
1ft YEAR, TURNIPS.							
	£.	s.	d.		£.	s.	d.
To ploughing 1½ inch deep	0	4	0	By turnips	4	0	0
Harrowing and raking	0	3	6				
Ploughing, harrowing and raking	0	7	6				
Ploughing and harrowing	0	5	0				
Making drills	0	2	6				
Leading refufe	0	2	6				
Manure, 6 loads, at 8s. per load	2	8	0				
Rent & affeffments	1	5	0				
Tythe	0	6	0				
Seed, and bufh harrowing	0	1	6				
Hoeing	0	1	0				
Ploughing 3 times	0	4	6				
	£5	11	0		£4	0	0

Dr. to EXPENCES.	Cr. by PRODUCE.

2d YEAR, BARLEY.

	£.	s.	d.		£.	s.	d.
To ploughing and harrowing	0	7	6	By barley, 4 quarters, at 1l. 5s. per quarter	5	0	0
Seed, 4 bushels	0	12	6				
Rent & assessments	1	5	0	Straw	1	0	0
Tythe	0	6	0				
Reaping and thrashing	0	12	0				
£3	3	0		£6	0	0	

3d YEAR PEAS.

	£.	s.	d.		£.	s.	d.
To ploughing, harrowing and raking	0	7	6	By 4 quarters of peas at 1l. 12s. per quarter	6	8	0
Ploughing, harrowing and raking	0	7	6	Straw	1	0	0
Making drills	0	2	6				
Manure, 4 loads, at 8s. per load	1	12	0				
Bush-harrowing	0	0	3				
Seed, 4 bushels	0	16	0				
3 times ploughing	0	4	6				
Reaping and thrashing	0	12	0				
Rent & assessments	1	5	0				
Tythe	0	6	0				
£5	13	3		£7	8	0	

4th YEAR, WHEAT.

	£.	s.	d.		£.	s.	d.
To scarifying and harrowing	0	3	0	By 3 quarters of wheat, 2l. 10s. per quarter	7	10	0
Ploughing and sowing	0	5	0	Straw	1	0	0
Seed-wheat, 3 bushels	0	18	9				
Rent & assessments	1	5	0				
Tythe	0	6	0				
Reaping & thrashing	0	15	0				
Clover-seed 10.b.	0	10	0				
£4	2	9		£8	10	0	

| Dr. to EXPENCES. | Cr. by PRODUCE. |

5th YEAR, CLOVER.

	£.	s.	d.		£.	s.	d.
To mowing and reaping	0	5	0	By 1½ ton of clover	6	0	0
Rent and assessments	1	5	0				
Tythe	0	6	0				
4 Loads manure, 8s. per load	1	12	0				
	£3	8	0		£6	0	0

6th YEAR, WHEAT.

	£.	s.	d.		£.	s.	d.
To ploughing and sowing	0	6	6	By 4 quarters of wheat, at 2l. 10s. per quarter	10	0	0
Seed, 3 bushels	0	18	9				
Reaping & thrashing	0	17	0	Straw	1	0	0
Rent and assessments	1	5	0				
Tythe	0	6	0				
	£3	13	3		£11	0	0

Total of the Cr. side	£ 43	18	0
Total of the Dr. ditto	25	11	3
Profit on one acre of land for six years	£ 17	6	9

'From the above calculations the reader will find, that by the old fyftem the farmer gets no more by his farm than 1*l.* 9*s.* 3*d.* profit upon one acre of land in fix years, or 4*s.* and 10½*d.* per acre yearly. The expence of labour is calculated higher in the above ftatement than it actually cofts him, or he could not pay his rent and maintain his family. Now the profit by the new fyftem is, in the fame fpace of time, 17*l.* 6*s.* 9*d.* which makes 2*l.* 17*s.* 9½*d.* yearly per acre, in the fix years rotation of crops— more than 100 per cent. in favour of the new fyftem.

There is in the above eftate an open pafture called the Horfe-car, which is let at 2*s.* 6*d.* per acre; and the tenants fay it is of no fervice to them: but, under proper cultivation, 5*l.* per acre yearly profit might be derived from it.— Then the tenant may well be furprifed when he is charged a new rent of 1*l.* 8*s.* per acre, though he now pays only 15*s.*; and indeed he is very high-rented according to the fyftem of agriculture he follows.

The lofs fuftained over two thoufand acres of land is 29,625*l.* in fix years. If that number
ber

ber of acres were let at 1*l.* 8*s.* per acre, there would be an advance of 13*s.* per acre, which would raife the fum of 7800*l.* for the tenants to pay in fix years. That fum deducted from 29,625*l.* will leave them a profit of 21,825*l.* Thefe calculations may ftagger the reader; but they are founded on facts. By a proper rotation of crops, the above profits would arife to landlord and tenant, even without the advantage of green fodder in fummer.

By a judicious management the farmers in Eaft Lothian are enabled to pay 3*l.* and 4*l.* per acre. If a man who lives by gardening, were to dig his land one year in three, and in the third year raife no crop, he would be confidered as a madman. But the two crops and a fallow are ftill worfe; as it robs the land of one third of its manure. This may be called opening the eyes of the landlord : but it is likewife greatly to the tenant's advantage.

SECTION

SECTION XLVI.

The Author's Opinion upon a General Inclosure of Commons ; proving Commons in their present State to be Nuisances, and a great Injury to the Community at large.

SOME knowledge of commons will most probably be allowed me. The reader may recollect that in the Introduction to this Work I informed him of my having lived at Afgafby in Lincolnshire : in consequence of the farm I there occupied, I enjoyed a right of common on the *East* and *West-Fen*; and I had ample opportunity of informing myself both as to the use and abuse of commons, from being one of the land-jury at a court held twice in every year, once for the purpose of hearing complaints, and once for imposing a fine for abuses, such as stocking without right, &c.

About Lady-day I sent into the West-Fen three hundred hogs (that is, sheep one year old, which have never been shorn). I hired a shepherd to attend them, and put them on the same walk the farmer used who occupied the farm prior to my coming to it. In less than a week,

in

in fpite of the care my own fhepherd certainly took, my fheep were difperfed over a fen confifting of twelve thoufand acres.

Their difperfion is eafily accounted for. There always are near commons an induftrious ingenious fet of men, whofe bufinefs it is to look after ftock for hire, and often for men who have no right of common. But, be that as it may, the better the ftock do under their care, the more employ they get. Therefore it becomes the intereft of thefe fhepherds to difturb every neighbouring flock, to make more room for fuch as are committed to them; and as they all have an intereft to do the fame thing, it becomes a combination of unjuft doers. Men of this defcription are awake while others of an oppofite difpofition fleep. Call upon any of thefe fellows in the day time; if you find them at all, it muft be in bed. They rife with the owl, and, like that bird, feek their prey by night. Late in the evening, one of thefe men mounts his horfe, and, accompanied by three or four dogs, goes amongft your fheep. He generally takes a few of thofe under his care, by way of excufe, and will drive half a dozen of them
into

into the middle of your flock, when they have lain down to reft for the night : he then fets the dogs a-barking; your pafture fheep, un-ufed to fuch alarms, rife in a fright and run dif-ferent ways. Having effectually difperfed the flock, he collects his own fheep, with the addi-tion of as many of yours as he can drive away with them; and he takes care to remove them fome miles from the fpot. When your fhep-herd comes to the ground in the morning, ex-pecting to find the fheep where he left them over night, he is moft fadly difappointed; fcarce any of the flock being to be found. He enquires of other fhepherds for his loft fheep. They, who are for the moft part what is term-ed *up to the bufinefs*, in return afk him the marks upon your fheep; and, having received from him fufficient information to know them, will direct him any way but the right. The man probably rides about the whole day without meeting with the objects of his fearch : both he and his horfe are forely fatigued by fruitlefs-ly wandering many miles. The peregrination is recommenced the next day, to as little pur-pofe; for by that time it is moft probable fome

part

part of the flock has been driven many miles
another way: but in the courfe of a week more
your fheep will be fo completely fcattered, that
you will have the fatisfaction, ride which way
you will, of feeing fome of them.

Your fhepherd may be one of whofe honefty
and capacity you before have had fufficient
proofs, and in this refpect no more to be bla-
med than yourfelf. He has only been a dupe
to thofe fellows who practife the trade of fheep-
herding for feveral mafters.

He tells you (which is moft probably true)
that he has taken every means in his power to
keep your fheep together; but they range fo
much that he muft have another horfe, and he
muft be allowed corn. By this time expences
run high: the horfe, if fold, would fetch lefs
by four pounds from the violent exercife he has
undergone; and you may add the fhepherd's
wages, and the keep of the horfe. But the
mifchief does not end here. In June the fheep
are to be wafhed, and, when brought upon the
farm, are found to have the fcab: twenty are
dead, and ten are miffing. You have two hundred and feventy fheep remaining of the three
hundred

hundred. Several extra expences are incurred from many of your sheep having been pounded, &c. Of those which died the skins are nearly destroyed by dogs.

Now, we will suppose these sheep to have been regularly joisted on good grass at 2d. per head per week, from Lady-day to the beginning of June—a period of ten weeks: that would amount to 37l. 10s. The shepherd's wages, at 12s. per week, comes to 6l. On the other hand, let us see what loss we may have suffered by the sheep put on the common during the same space of time.

	£.	s.	d.
The shepherd's wages, at 12s. per week, will be - - -	6	0	0
Corn for two horses, each 8s. per week - - - -	8	0	0
Twenty sheep dead, at 25s. each	25	0	0
Loss on two horses decreased in value - - - -	8	0	0
276 sheep curing of scab, at 3d. per sheep - - -	3	9	0
276 ditto decreased in value from common keep, 5s. -	69	0	0
Fines for sheep pounded, &c. only estimated at 5s. - -	0	5	0
Losses and Expences -	£119	14	0

The

The whole expence of joisting,
or properly keeping the sheep
will be 37*l*. 10*s*. at 3*d*. per head
per week : and adding the expence of the shepherd, which
is certainly over rated at 6*l*.
you have a total of   43 10 0
We will allow two sheep lost by
death or accident, at 25*s*.   2 10 0
Suppose twenty-two skins, as they
must have been torn by dogs,
or otherwise damaged, sold for   3 10 0
                                    ———————
                             £49 10 0

By subtracting the 49*l*. 10*s*. from 119*l*. 14*s*.
you will have a balance of 70*l*. 4*s*. which is the
least profit you will reap from the difference of
keeping three hundred sheep in a proper manner instead of turning them upon the common.
I have chosen the ten best weeks in the whole
year for the purpose of stocking the commons
mentioned ; for, if you send sheep there later,
you will be still a greater loser. The commons
will then be covered with innumerable flocks
of geese.

                                        In

In June numbers of cattle and horfes are turned loofe upon them ; by which as much is loft as by fheep. The horfes get full of bots, or the fmall needle worms, or, in dry fummers, of fand. A horfe of mine, which had run upon the common in fummer, died, and I was defirous of knowing what occafioned his death.— On opening him, upwards of a peck of fand was found in his great ftomach or bag. In mild winters, horfes which have run the fummer in the fens do beft there in winter ; for, as all horfes feeding on low grounds get the bots or grubs, which are natives of fuch grounds ; fo, while the horfes continue there eating green food, the bots and worms do him little mifchief, as they will prefer that kind of nutriment to what they might get by preying upon the animal. But when the horfe quits grafs, and is taken to dry meat, the bots and worms begin to devour his vifcera. They gnaw his inteftines, they confume the chyle, and prevent the proper fupply to the blood, which affumes much the fame appearance as the blood of rotten fheep. His head begins to fwell; and fo do his

his legs, and fome get what is called the *felteric*.
The greater the quantity of corn and dry meat
you give him, the worfe he becomes ; and the
only method left to fave him is to keep him on
grafs. If you have carrots or potatoes, they
would anfwer much bettter than corn or any
dry food. I have loft feveral horfes by this
fort of diforder : from the defire of collecting
manure, I have put them into a ftraw-fold,
which I now know to be a certain method of
defpatching them quickly. Chopped ftraw,
which I have hitherto fo ftrongly recommended
as the moft wholefome and cheapeft food, is
here rank poifon—a proof that there is no rule
without an exception, I have felt it to my coft.
When any of my horfes died of this diftemper,
or, in fact, of any other, I generally opened
them by way of practice; and I have frequently found the principal ftomach or *bag*, as the
farriers term it, nearly eaten through by thefe
deftructive vermin : none which died of the
bots but had the coat of the ftomach nearly deftroyed. If you turn beafts upon a common,
at a year old, and give them ftraw in the winter, they will increafe in age, but very little in

fize

fize when three years old: confequently there is little gain.

If I wanted to ftock the Fen, I fhould prefer doing fo without having a right; for, by applying to one of the Fen fhepherds, he would take a decent number at a cheap rate. I have known men have ftock in the Fen who had neither houfe nor land in the county. A Fen fhepherd will render the qualified man's right of little value; and, whilft he will affift in driving away ftock legally put on the common, he will, if properly fee'd, be particularly careful of the property of ftrangers. Now, were this common inclofed, it would produce an incredible quantity of corn, to the great benefit of the country at large : it would feed a vaft number of cattle ; and it would alfo afford employment for a number of perfons who now follow little bufinefs but that of thieving.

The draining of the fwamps in fo large a tract of flat country is a matter of the utmoft importance in refpect to the health of the inhabitants : and the neceffary dividing of the land (fuppofing the whole to be inclofed) would by ditches nearly effect the purpofe, and do it

effectually

effectually with the affiftance of a main drain, and an outfall.

I have mentioned the beft common in England : and even that common, I infift upon it, is no better than a nuifance. Commons are harbours and nurferies for thieves. I was on the jury when three men were indicted at York affizes for ftealing fome fheep from commons in Craven : and it came out in proof upon trial, that thefe men had dealt largely, though not poffeffed of a capital. Their trade was thieving : and they were ingenious men in their way, all of one family, father and two fons. The eldeft fon paffed for a jobber in fheep : and the father, with the youngeft fon, lived nine miles diftant from him. The eldeft fon collected a tolerable flock by ftealing a fingle fheep from thofe he was difpofed to favour ; two or three from other people, and fo on. He would likewife buy a few, then mix them all together, and drive them to the old man's farm. Thefe fheep were but of fmall value, worth from five to feven fhillings each ; which deterred the owners from incurring the expence of a profecution : although many of the fufferers

ers knew where to find their property. These men therefore followed the trade of sheep-stealing with impunity. When one of the owners was asked by the Judge, "why he did not not swear to a certain sheep when first he discovered it in the possession of the old man;" he answered, "he was afraid of the consequences." On the Judge's enquiring what were the consequences he meant; he replied, "that he was afraid of incurring a heavy expence." They were all convicted.

Now, were these commons inclosed, such men as have been just described could make no excuse for trespassing upon a person's property; it would be more difficult to get amongst another man's flock of sheep, and they would be much more easily detected after a robbery. Prevention is allowed to be better than punishment: the breed of thieves—a breed with which this country is overstocked—would be diminished by inclosures: by inclosures would the national wealth be augmented, and of course benefit accrue to the community at large.

SECTION

SECTION XLVII.

*Experiments in Agriculture, according to the
New System.*

IT will be remembered, that I have before
recommended fowing the garden peas in preference to the field peas.   They are more likely to produce a good crop, becaufe they are
more hardy than field peas.   I put the early
Charlton pearls, and the dwarf marrow-fats in
the ground nearly at one time, and in the fame
manner in every refpect as the Hafting pea,
which I have found to get forward fafter than
any other field pea.   Garden-peas of all forts
will, like turnips, thrive much better in the
open field than in a garden ; and the method
laid down under the head *Pea Fallow* is much
fuperior to what is generally practifed by the
gardeners.

I have had cabbages much more forward,
and better in every refpect, than what are to be
found in gardens: at the fame time they were
treated, as explained under *Cabbage-Fallow.*—
Were this mode of culture attended to, it
would

would create a greater plenty of vegetables, and in all probability reduce the price.

What has been faid of peas and cabbages, is equally applicable to beans. But the rooks are fo fond of them, and deftroy fuch quantities, that the farmer may fometimes be difappointed of a good crop—a circumftance which has happened to me ; for I have found it impoffible to keep thefe voracious birds off, although I had a woman conftantly in the field for the purpofe.

I had an excellent crop of onions, fown broadcaft, entirely managed by the plough and harrows.

The greateft produce of wheat I have had has been upon fallow, from fowing under furrow as near $1\frac{1}{2}$ inch deep as it was poffible to plough. The method is as follows : Harrow the land very fine, and then make a mark with the plough upon the place where the ridge is intended to be. Then fow the wheat, and turn a furrow over it. Then continue fowing down the furrow after the plough. A boy or a girl is much better than a man or a woman for any of this fort of work. By being nearer to the

ground they are lefs liable to fcatter the feed
to one fide of the furrow; for, if the wind
blows, it is apt to mifs the part intended. A
boy or girl will fow an acre for 6*d*.; and if the
ploughman be attentive, they may be made to
do it in a very regular manner. It is eafy to
afcertain the proper quantity for one furrow.
Knowing the length of the lands and the width
of the furrow intended to be ploughed, you
may calculate the number of furrows in each
acre. Then dividing by the number of furrows the quantity of wheat intended for each
acre, the quotient will be the exact quantity for
each furrow. There is a drill for this fort of
fowing, but I have not feen it act. There is
only one thing I diflike in this method, viz.
the danger of the ploughman's covering the
wheat too deep; which is a very great fault.
For the wheat either rots in the land and never
gets up, or is liable to canker during the winter,
in the fame manner as you will fee celery in a
garden. The wire-worm often bears the blame.
I have very minutely examined thofe plants
that are eaten in two : and in the winter I have
very feldom found the worm; but very frequently

quently the plant cut in two by the froft and wet weather : and it may be obferved that it is moftly in very fevere winters that wheat is deftroyed by what is called wire-worms. Laft winter I had nine acres all fown with the fame fort of wheat; but the land differently treated. Of the nine acres there had been one acre and a half of peas for podding; with four loads of manure on it. In the midft of thefe, half an acre of beans, with four loads of manure.— There had been four acres of potatoes, with eighteen loads upon each acre—two acres and a half of peas, with four loads of manure per acre—and half an acre fown broad-caft with field peas, and fix loads of manure on it. The wire-worm, fo called, was more or lefs deftruct-ive in proportion, as more or lefs manure was laid on each part of the field. Where the beans had grown in the middle of the peas, there was a remarkably fine crop; but on both fides, in fome places, where the land was the moft wet by nature, although very well griped and drain-ed, more than half of the wheat was deftroyed from want of a fufficient quantity of manure to give vigour to the plants. Beans are generally

fuppofed

supposed to impoverish land more than peas; yet, in the above experiment, the bean-land, although potatoes, another impoverisher, had grown among the beans, produced by the assistance of the manure the best wheat. Indeed, on tillage land, I have always found good manure properly applied to bear crops accordingly.

Experiments on a Farm at Sprodborough.

In the year 1791 I had only nine acres of land, on which I kept nine horses, two cows, fourteen sheep, and one hundred and thirty pigs; all fed with grains, except the sheep. The sheep, notwithstanding their being intermixed with the rest of the stock, became very fat. The lambs I sold at 21*s*. per head; and some of them were afterwards sold for breeding at 2*l*. 12*s*. 6*d*. a piece. One of the cows cost 11*l*. with her calf in May: I sold her in October for 13*l*, after taking her milk:

In the year 1792 I took a farm consisting of twenty-eight acres of pasture, at 4l. per acre—eighteen acres of tillage-land laid down with clover, at 28*s*. per acre—ten acres in grass, at

26*s*.

26s. per acre—two acres in wheat, at 26s. per acre. The rent of the new farm was 152l. 6s. per year : that of the nine acres of grafs 3l. per acre. The whole was tytheable, except the twenty-eight acres of pasture. My method of grazing and cropping was as follows : The pasture of twenty-eight acres used to be regularly stocked by my predeceffor with nineteen beasts and four horses, but no sheep. I put into it twenty beasts, fourteen horses, twenty ewes, and twenty-seven lambs. Finding it overstocked, I took in the nine acres of meadows. I fattened forty beasts in that summer. The twenty ewes and twenty-seven lambs paid 50l. 16s.—See the Agricultural Reports of Yorkshire. The eighteen acres of clover were mown once—the ten acres of sward ploughed up and sown with oats—Clover bad—oats middling. Two acres of wheat, bad.

In the year 1793—In the feeding-pasture fourteen cows, thirty ewes, forty-fix lambs, and fourteen horses, which all did well as before.—The eighteen acres, wheat; bad, only 210 bushels—ten acres peas, good; two acres of turnips good; fold at five guineas per acre.

In

In 1794—In the feeding-pasture fourteeen cows, fourteen horses, fifty ewes, and sixty-four lambs. All did well—the lambs uncommonly good. In the eighteen acres, six acres of potatoes in drills three feet asunder—the sorts set, the kidney, ox-noble, manly, champion, red-apple, white-apple, and lemon, which produced a good crop—the ox-noble, ninety sacks per acre ; the manly, eighty ditto ; the red-apple, eighty ditto ; the white, seventy ditto ; the kidney, fifty ditto ; the lemon, forty ditto. At one corner of the six acres was a piece of sward I took from the high road, dug by the spade, and set with potatoes. Ten square yards were planted in the lazy-bed method, and ten yards square by digging the land and setting in drills, as is usual ; the land being all manured. The lazy-bed method raised sixteen stone four pounds : the drills at eighteen inches asunder, seven stone five pounds. From this experiment I have improved much in the manner of setting potatoes. The other twelve acres oats, bad ; The ten acres and two acres being put into one field ; six acres of wheat, good : six acres barley, middling. The nine acres remained meadow.

In the year 1795 the ufual ftock in the feeding-pafture. In this year I had a lamb that weighed twenty pounds per quarter when fix months old—all the reft uncommonly fat. Nine acres, meadow. Of the eighteen-acres-field, fix acres (where potatoes had grown the preceding year) wheat good. The wheat was fown under furrow an inch and half deep; except one acre, two inches and a half deep, which yielded lefs by nine bufhels per acre—the quantity fown four bufhels on part of the five acres; on the other part, three bufhels—the latter the beft wheat; but not much difference in yield—the quantity thirty bufhels per acre. In 1795 the fmall worm did much damage in the wheat crops in the ear: mine was much affected. Six acres potatoes, fet every furrow, as directed in this Work—four acres of the fix fown with rape among the potatoes. The ox-noble potatoe was planted on five of the acres; and the black-apple on one of them—thefe bad: the ox-noble, where the rape was not fown, as good as ever I faw; one hundred and ninety facks per acre—where the rape was fown with them, only fifty facks. The

black

black apple, although no rape was fown among them, produced only thirty facks. The black-apples fuit wet land, being remarkably hard. I found, that by fowing rape among them I had loft one hundred and forty facks per acre; and I received only 2*l.* 10*s.* from feeding fheep with the rape. The other fix acres wheat, with the fame quantity of manure as the fix a-cres of potatoes, and three ploughings after the oats—produce eight bufhels lefs than on the fix acres where potatoes had preceded the wheat. The twelve-acre field, oats—eight bufhels per acre fown—the beft crop I ever faw of the Tartarian fort—fix feet high regu-larly, and the thickeft on the ground perhaps ever feen.

In the year 1796 I had in the feeding-pafture fourteen cows, fourteen horfes, fifty ewes, and fixty-feven lambs. The fuperfluous grafs was mown the greateft part of fummer, and given to the horfes in the ftable. I found the cows and fheep do much better. There was a Scotch cow amongft them, which the May twelve months before coft five guineas. She was with calf—fold her calf for feventeen
fhillings

fhillings when fat. The cow was a good milk-
er, and was milked within fix weeks of her being killed—weighed thirty-fix ftone, nine ftone
of fat—fold for fixteen guineas. I have found,
from repeated trials, that the fmall Scotch
cows confume, on an average, one fifth lefs than
a large cow of the Tees-water kind. This
year I had a calf, which at the age of thirteen
weeks weighed nineteen ftone twelve pounds
and a half, and had fucked no other cow but
its own mother.—I increafed my farm by nine
acres, which had had oats the year before upon flag-land or fward ploughed up. I raifed
on thefe nine acres the following crops : one
acre and half of Charlton peas, very good—
one rood of Windfor beans, bad—one rood of
long-podded beans; bad crop, the rooks had
eaten the feed. The long-pods yielded fifteen
bufhels and a half; the Windfor, nine bufhels
and a half. Potatoes under them, twenty-five
facks—Two acres and an half of Hafting peas
drilled; very good, forty bufhels per acre.
Half an acre of field-peas fown broad-caft:
good, produce fifteen bufhels. Four acres of
potatoes; produce one hundred and ninety
facks

facks per acre. In the eighteen-acres field, fix
acres wheat, where potatoes grew the year before; good, forty-eight bufhels per acre—
twelve acres of oats, middling. The twelve-
acre field, wheat, good; thirty-two bufhels
per acre. Thefe crops (except the oats, which
were kept to cut for horfes, cows, &c.) were
fold on the ground for ten guineas per acre,
and paid the purchafer well. I had all the ftraw,
chaff, &c.

In 1797, in the month of May, I quitted
this farm. At that time the nine acres, where
potatoes, beans, &c. had grown the preceding
year, were in wheat : every other land drilled
by Mr. Cook himfelf, with one bufhel per acre ;
the reft fown broad-caft with three bufhels per
acre—the produce of that fown broad-caf:
about three to one more than that of the dril-
ed. There was a very great crop of wheat by
the broad-caft. Of the eighteen acres, one
acre and a half in cabbages, and potatoes under them—two acres in early potatoe —five
acres and a half in garden peas—two acres in
Hafting peas—fix acres of potatoes, ox-no-
bles—one acre of long-podded beans, with po-

tatoes under them. The crop was fold at 200*l.*
in the month of May.

The greateft part of the above experiments
being treated of feparately in other parts of this
Work, I have here only concifely ftated the rotation of crops. It may not be unneceffary to
obferve, that, at the time I quitted the farm,
the eighteen acres field was a perfect garden,
with fcarcely a weed in it : but in the month
of July a perfect wildernefs ; and I may venture to affert that, for want of beftowing from
5*l.* to 10*l.* on the different crops, there was
100*l.* lefs profit derived from the field, than
might have been expected if proper management had not been wanting. Moreover the
land is in a rude improper ftate for wheat ; and
in the old mode of agriculture will require a
fallow. Therefore it will make the difference
of the following fum, in eighteen acres of land,
in two years.

Lofs

Lofs for want of proper management this
   year 100l. and expences of four ploughings to make the land ready for wheat
   next year, 24l. 12s.   £ 124 12 0

Lofs of eighteen acres of wheat, at fix
   quarters per acre, at 56s. per quarter,
   which might have grown on the land
   next fummer, without fallow; deducting for feed and fowing 18l. 18s. for
   ploughing, 5l. 6s. and for reaping 9l.   179 10 0

                                304 2 0

Deduct the fum faved   10 10 0

Lofs in two years by an improper method of managing, on eighteeen
   acres   £ 293 12 0

The above ftatement plainly fhews how plans
of improvement may be rendered abortive by
neglect. It is fomething like building a houfe
and never finifhing it. I have known the late
Mr. Bakewell's fheep bought by different people; and for want of care and management
they have foon degenerated.

SECTION

SECTION XLVIII.

The proper Sort of Pigs ; and the best Method of Breeding them.

PIGS are of various kinds ; and the choice of the sort should be regulated by the treatment they are to receive. The Chinese breed with short ears are most profitable, when suffered to range at full liberty in woods : and even in pastures, they will not only live, but get fat with grass ; but they will not thrive in the sty or fold with grains or inferior food.

I tried some experiments on the Chinese pigs. I had a most remarkably fat one of that breed. A gentleman who saw it, and who was famous for breeding that kind, sent me a boar and two gelts. I kept the sows for some time in a fold, with from fifty to a hundred of a sort, which will be described hereafter : they were larger than the Chinese, and weighed from twenty to twenty-five stone each. Mine, though so much larger than the Chinese breed, became fat, whilst they remained lean. I then moved them, and gave them better food ; when they soon became nice pigs, and paid well for the meat

they

they ate. But although one was killed at the age of three years, she weighed only ten stone: the other was killed when four years old, and she weighed only twelve stone. It is to be observed, that the last-mentioned one was always the largest: it was not its being one year older than the other that gave it the advantage in weight; for these fort of pigs soon arrive at their full growth, and the increafe of weight is then according as the animal is more or lefs fat.

I have always found the Berkshire pigs with a crofs of the Chinefe the best for all ufes — Such pigs, when full grown, will weigh thirty stone with a moderate quantity of food. I put up a very poor fow, taken from her first litter of pigs, and which had been fuffered to remain fo long as to leave her fcarce any thing but fkin and bone: however, I determined to fatten her, becaufe she had got a trick of killing fowls.—— The highest price bid me for her in this condition was one guinea and a half. I gave her nine bushels of peas at 3s. 6d. per bufhel. When killed, she weighed feventeen stone, and at that time pork fit for bacon was worth from 7s. to 7s. 6d. per stone: therefore, at 7s. per ftone only, there was a clear profit of 2*l.* 16*s.* for the trouble of feeding. I have had many more proofs of the extraordinary thrift of pigs of this fort, which I originally bred from a Berkfhire fow and a Chinefe boar. The firft of them, a fow fed and killed at Burton-upon-Trent, was twenty four inches wide upon the back, and weighed forty-feven ftone. They may be faid to grow until they are two years old : but the growth of pigs, like that of other animals, depends upon the manner in which they are kept.

It will be found that, although pigs in fome cafes are the moft profitable animals, yet they feldom will pay for corn or any other kind of food which the farmer can difpofe of at a good market. They eat what no other animals will touch : therefore, with a trifling addition of better food, they will thrive very well. To keep them on corn, the expence would foon exceed the profit expected. In fact, I know of no animal except a horfe that will pay for corn.— See Section XXXI. page 144. and Section XXXVIII. page 178.

SECTION

SECTION XLIX.

Great Use of Pigs in Fold-yards.

PIGS not only pick up the refuse of the fold-yard, and thrive upon it; but, besides depositing their own dung, they rout the litter about in such a manner as to break and shorten the straw, from which, by chewing it, they derive nourishment. By routing and trampling over the yard, they mingle the materials, and cause the manure to imbibe an equal quantity of moisture, in such a manner as could scarcely be done by any other means; thus bringing it speedily to perfection. I do not now speak of the Chinese breed: they are of little use in this respect, as they rout very little. Strong or large pigs of the Berkshire or of the long-eared kind are the fittest for making manure in the fold-yard: And to cause them to do this properly, they ought to be kept in good condition, and one day in every week nothing given them to eat, by which means they would effectually turn the manure; for in a short time pigs will be to feed in the folds, the thrashing machine will leave nothing in the straw for them to eat.

END OF THE FIRST VOLUME.